MANUSCRIPT, SOCIETY
AND BELIEF IN EARLY
CHRISTIAN EGYPT

MANUSCRIPT, SOCIETY AND BELIEF IN EARLY CHRISTIAN EGYPT

COLIN H. ROBERTS

HON. D.LITT.

Fellow of the Academy

THE SCHWEICH LECTURES
OF THE BRITISH ACADEMY
1977

LONDON · *Published for* THE BRITISH ACADEMY
by THE OXFORD UNIVERSITY PRESS

This book has been printed digitally and produced in a standard specification
in order to ensure its continuing availability

OXFORD
UNIVERSITY PRESS

Great Clarendon Street, Oxford OX2 6DP

Oxford University Press is a department of the University of Oxford.
It furthers the University's objective of excellence in research, scholarship,
and education by publishing worldwide in

Oxford New York

Auckland   Cape Town Dar es Salaam   Hong Kong   Karachi
Kuala Lumpur Madrid Melbourne Mexico City   Nairobi
New Delhi Shanghai Taipei Toronto
With offices in
Argentina Austria Brazil Chile Czech Republic France Greece
Guatemala Hungary Italy Japan South Korea Poland Portugal
Singapore Switzerland Thailand Turkey Ukraine Vietnam

Oxford is a registered trade mark of Oxford University Press
in the UK and in certain other countries

Published in the United States
by Oxford University Press Inc., New York

ISBN 0-19-725982-0

Antony Rowe Ltd., Eastbourne

PREFACE

IT is a pleasure to thank both the President and Council of the British Academy for the invitation to give the Schweich Lectures in the spring of 1977 and the President and Fellows of St. John's College, Oxford, who in continuation of a generosity and consideration that now goes back over more than fifty years elected me to a Senior Research Fellowship for the years 1974–6. This provided me with both the incentive and facilities to put together scattered notes I had accumulated on the subject matter of these lectures, to re-think some old problems, and to discover some new ones in an attempt to link palaeography and papyrology with the history of the early church in Egypt.

The printed text is substantially that of the lectures; to this I have added notes, sometimes discursive, and a few appendices. These will, I hope, make clear my indebtedness to other scholars, but there is one acknowledgement which calls for particular mention. The publication in 1976 by the Abbé J. van Haelst of his catalogue of Christian papyri (referred to on p. ix) has simplified my task, makes it easier for the reader to discover more about a particular text, and has placed all students of early Christianity in his debt.

December 1978   C.H.R.

CONTENTS

ABBREVIATIONS

Publications of papyri are referred to by the standard abbreviations, a list of which may conveniently be found in E. G. Turner's *Greek Papyri: an Introduction* (Oxford, 1968). For biblical and other theological papyri, whether Christian or Jewish, a cross-reference is given to the Abbé van Haelst's invaluable *Catalogue des papyrus litteraires juifs et chrétiens* (Paris, 1976) which gives a brief description of and some bibliographical information on each text; it is cited as 'H', followed by the number in the catalogue.

Other abbreviations employed are as follows:

Archiv	*Archiv für Papyrusforschung*
CPJ	V. A. Tcherikover, A. Fuks, M. Stern, *Corpus Papyrorum Judaicarum*
GLH	C. H. Roberts, *Greek Literary Hands* (Oxford, 1956)
GMAW	E. G. Turner, *Greek Manuscripts of the Ancient World* (Oxford, 1971)
HTR	*Harvard Theological Review*
JEA	*Journal of Egyptian Archaeology*
JTS	*Journal of Theological Studies*
Turner, *Typology*	E. G. Turner, *The Typology of the Early Codex* (University of Pennsylvania, 1977)
ZPE	*Zeitschrift für Papyrologie und Epigraphik*
ZTNW	*Zeitschrift für die neutestament liche Wissenschaft*

I

THE EVIDENCE OF THE PAPYRI

THE obscurity that veils the early history of the Church in Egypt and that does not lift until the beginning of the third century constitutes a conspicuous challenge to the historian of primitive Christianity. The nature of the problem is apparent when we recall that Alexandria was not only the greatest Greek city in the world and the centre of scholarship but as the home of the largest Jewish community outside Palestine would have been a primary target for the Christian mission, and then set against these considerations the jejune and scrappy references in our literary sources. These sources, of which the principal is the fourth century historian Eusebius, have been examined and re-examined by Church historians and never to more effect than by Adolf Harnack;[1] but for the first two centuries there is little enough to be gleaned from them.

If we look, as we reasonably might, for illumination to the documentary papyri of the first three centuries, we shall be disappointed; the few allusions there are in letters and other documents were garnered by H. I. Bell and later by J. van Haelst[2] and little to be added to their lists has come to light

[1] *Die Mission und Ausbreitung des Christentums*[4] (Leipzig, 1924), pp. 705 ff.

[2] H. I. Bell, *Evidences of Christianity in Egypt during the Roman period* in *HTR*, 37. (1944), pp. 185 ff., on which see the present writer in *JEA* 40 (1954), p. 92: J. van Haelst, *Les Sources papyrologiques concernant l'Église en Egypte à l'époque de Constantin* in *Proc. XII Int. Congress of Papyrology* (Toronto, 1970), pp. 499 ff., which covers the years 270–350. In contrast to Bell (p. 197) who regards one letter of *c.* 200 (P. Harris 107) as certainly Christian, an opinion which I share, van Haelst (p. 503) finds the silence of the documents before 250 to be complete. The interpretation of certain monotheistic expressions in a Christian sense in letters of the second and third century by M. Naldini in *Cristianesimo in Egitto* (Florence, 1968) has been subjected to trenchant and convincing criticism by E. Wipszycka in *The Journal of Juristic Papyrology* 18 (1974), pp. 203 sq., who points out that the growth of monotheism in the third century led to the creation of a religious language common to Christians, Jews, and some pagans. In his analysis four of Naldini's letters are deleted as non-Christian, thirty-one are classified as *dubia*, and a further sixteen are redated to after the middle of the fourth century.

Since van Haelst wrote, I have noted two additions to his list, P. Oxy. xxxvi. 2785. a Christian letter of introduction of the early fourth century, and P. Oxy. xlii. 3035 of 28 Febr. 256, an order for the arrest of a certain Petosarapis, described as Χριστιανός (the earliest instance of the word in the papyri). Support for van Haelst's view that the background of priests, readers, etc. in the late third and early fourth centuries is that of the urban élite, well-to-do and Greek in culture, may be found in the name Κόλων. According to Eusebius, *H.E.* vi. 46, this was the name of the Bishop of Hermopolis in the middle of the third century; the Greek name is rare in the papyri and I have found two instances only, one of which

in recent years. The purpose of these lectures is to discover whether the Christian literary papyri, both Biblical and other, can be called on as evidence for the history and character of the Church in Egypt and whether there may not be some cross-fertilization between these papyri and our literary sources that might result in a revision of some of the conclusions of modern scholarship.[1]

After, as I hope, the relevance and limits of this evidence have been established, this first chapter will look closely at some of the earliest Christian texts to see what can be learnt about those who wrote them and those who used them. It will be largely a discursive survey of the material and will inevitably traverse much familiar ground. The second will be devoted to one particular problem: the significance for both the history and the theology of the early Church of the abbreviations in our earliest manuscripts of certain divine or sacred names which under the rubric of *nomina sacra* have long been the subject of palaeographical study. The third chapter will be concerned, in the light of the findings of the first two chapters, with the growth and character of the Egyptian church in the first three centuries down to approximately the death of Constantine, as seen in its relations with the Jews, with the Gnostics, and with the native Egyptian population.

It may be asked why, given the relative frequency of Christian literary texts—there are some 150 that approximately fall within our period[2]—there are so few references, and those sometimes ambivalent, in the documents. The answer lies partly in the nature of the material, partly in the relations between Church and State. While the Jews had a recognized political status and were classified e.g. for purposes of taxation as distinct from Greeks and Egyptians, there was no ground for distinguishing a Christian as such from anyone else and often very good reasons why he should not draw attention to himself.

(B.G.U. xii, 2133. 1 refers to a bearer of the name as $\gamma]\upsilon\mu(\ )]$ $\beta o\upsilon\lambda(\ )'E\rho\mu[o\upsilon\pi\delta\lambda\epsilon\omega\varsigma]$ in the late third century. We may see here a parallel to the son of the councillor of Arsinoe who is recorded as living as a hermit in Kerkesephis (P. Würz. 16).

[1] A brief statement of this case was set out in my *Early Christianity in Egypt: Three Notes* (*JEA* 40 (1954), pp. 92 ff.).

[2] If the pre-Christian Jewish texts are omitted from the index of papyri earlier than Constantine in van Haelst's *Catalogue*, the number is still slightly higher than the figure I have given. This is partly because his list includes Jewish as well as Christian manuscripts (for these see Appendix I), partly because it errs if at all on the side of inclusiveness; thus it includes a few magical texts in which Christian terms occur but which are not necessarily of Christian origin (see Appendix IV) as well as a text such as no. 553, the Maxims of Ahiqar (*alias* the Aesop Romance) which, though of interest to students of the Bible, is certainly not Christian. To his index should be added P. Oxy. xli. 2949, a fragment of an apocryphal Gospel.

If allusions to Christianity in private letters of the period are few, there was little occasion, as Bell pointed out,[1] in the ordinary letter to mention religious belief. We have, after all, several thousand papyri of classical literature, but singularly few references in the documents to intellectual life.[2] The word Χριστιανός is first found in the papyri in an order from the President of the Council of Oxyrhynchus dated A.D. 256 instructing a village headman and the overseers of the peace to arrest a certain Petosarapis son of Horus, described as a Christian;[3] allusions to the practices and terminology of the new creed would not be in place until it became a publicly recognized religion, reflected in the formulae of the state and of everyday life.

Here a parallel from another minority group may be pertinent in more ways than one. Among the sub-literary papyri is a group of texts dating from the first three centuries of our era to which modern scholars have given the designation of 'Acts of the Alexandrian (or Pagan) Martyrs';[4] for the most part they are accounts of the resistance of the Greek patriots of Alexandria to the Roman supremacy and often take the form of a trial before Emperor or Prefect. While based on and including one or two genuine documents (notably of the first fifty years of Roman rule), the texts, especially the later ones, are often embroidered in a novelistic manner. This 'pamphleting literature', as E. G. Turner has called it,[5] had a wide, if surely clandestine, circulation; limited as its appeal must have been, specimens of it have been found in the Arsinoite, in Oxyrhynchus, and (probably) in Panopolis. From our present standpoint three of its characteristics are worth noting, its clandestine nature and minority interest apart. Firstly, it is evidence of the very close relations subsisting between Alexandrians and their kinsmen or friends hundreds of miles away in Middle or Upper Egypt; secondly, many of these texts are written in a style 'midway between cursive and literary';[6]

---

[1] Op. cit., pp. 198–9.

[2] For one of the rare exceptions see below, p. 4, n. 2, and for a recent and important addition to the category see the text published with full commentary by P. J. Parsons, *The Grammarian's Complaint* in *Collectanea Papyrologica* ii, pp. 409 ff.   [3] See p. 1, n. 2 above.

[4] In general see H. A. Musurillo, *The Acts of the Pagan Martyrs* (Oxford, 1954). See also E. G. Turner's introduction to P. Oxy. 2435 and P. J. Parsons in *Studia Papyrologica* 15 (1976), p. 97 and his introductions to P. Oxy. xlii, 3020 and 3021.

[5] *GMAW*, p. 96. For the connection with Panopolis, see E. G. Turner, *Greek Papyri* (Oxford, 1968), p. 52.

[6] So Turner on P. Oxy. xxv, 2435. Thirteen out of the twenty papyri in Musurillo's collection are described as being written in a 'quasi-literary' or 'semi-cursive' hand (see Musurillo, *op. cit.*, p. 223).

lastly, there is no reference to this literature in any papyrus letter or routine document, and until the first texts were published we had no inkling of its existence.

With this analogy in mind, we shall not be inclined to accept the view of some scholars that until the third century Christianity was confined to Alexandria[1] when Christian manuscripts of second century date have been found in Middle and Upper Egypt. To argue that these early texts were either introduced much later into provincial Egypt or have been wildly misdated is a solution of the problem that does not stand up to examination. There is abundant evidence of a close and continuous relationship between the Greeks of Alexandria and the Greek middle class in the provincial towns and villages at all levels—economic, cultural, and personal.[2] One instance we have just noted in connection with the Acts of the Pagan Martyrs; to select one other out of the many available, in the Fayûm village of Philadelphia 325 Philadelphians were registered in the first century as resident outside the village and of these no fewer than 64 were resident in Alexandria, and, as the tax register is incomplete, the total may well have been higher.[3] Furthermore, our sources indicate that Jews kept in touch with their coreligionists in the provinces;[4] why should Christians, especially if converts from Judaism, have behaved differently?

[1] e.g. G. Bardy, *Pour l'histoire de l'école d'Alexandrie* in *Vivre et Penser* 2 (1942), pp. 80 ff. So too van Haelst (see p. 1, n. 2 above) concludes that there were no Christians in the χώρα before the middle of the third century because of the absence of documentary evidence; accepting the editor's date for P. Yale 1 (see below, p. 13), he has to argue that it was written in Alexandria and later taken to the χώρα. However, in a footnote to his *Catalogue* (p. 409), he accepts the existence of the early literary papyri as evidence for the history of the Church.
    On different grounds, W. Telfer in the *Journal of Ecclesiastical History*, 3 (1951), pp. 2 ff., concluded that 'Egyptian Christianity in A.D. 190 was thus confined to the city (sc. Alexandria) and its environs'. For a criticism of this view (dependent on the fact that in the Paschal controversy the Bishop of Alexandria is mentioned, but not other bishops), see my article referred to on p. 1, n. 2 above.
[2] See E. G. Turner on *Roman Oxyrhynchus* in *JEA* 38 (1952), pp. 78–93 and id. *Scribes and Scholars of Oxyrhynchus* in M.P.E.R. N.S. 5, pp. 141 ff. The ownership of estates by Alexandrians in Egypt south of the Delta was at its maximum in the second century A.D.; see M. A. H. el Abbadi in *Proc. XIV Congress of Papyrology* (London, 1975), p. 96. For a family of Roman citizens who were also high officials in Alexandria and owned estates in Oxyrhynchus and possibly in the Arsinoite and Hermopolite nomes as well, see P. Oxy. xliv. 3197.
    A fascinating glimpse of the cultural link between Alexandria and Oxyrhynchus in the early second century A.D. is provided by P. Primi 11; in this the writer, probably a cultured bookseller, sends a note to a friend who shares his interest in philosophy, attaching a list of books on Stoicism he has had copied in Alexandria (cf. U. Wilcken in *Archiv* 12 (1937), p. 80).
[3] P. Princeton i. 14; see A. E. Hanson, *Poll Tax in Philadelphia and P. Mich. Inv. 887* in *Proc. XIV Congress of Papyrology*, pp. 149 ff. One example of wider contacts may be given; in A.D. 72/3 out of 143 males registered in one quarter of the town of Arsinoe three were resident in Rome and one in India (P. Lond. ii. 260: cf. *Stud. Pap.* i. 74).
[4] See V. A. Tcherikover and A. Fuks, *CPJ*, *Prolegomena* pp. 68 and 86 ff. with the documents relating to the Jews of Alexandria from Abusir-el-Meleq, nos. 142 ff.

In the third place, there is the evidence of the texts themselves, to be looked at more closely later on; there we may note that at least two of the second-century texts are indisputably of local origin and that though opinions may differ about the date of a particular text, the general basis for our palaeographical judgments, resting on a very large amount of evidence, is reasonably secure.[1]

It is scarcely credible that a disused local register should be carried several hundred miles to Alexandria to have the verso of the roll inscribed with a Christian text and then be returned to the province where it originated.[2] Nor is the theory plausible even if we limit ourselves to the literary evidence. This testifies to the existence of a strongly Christianized form of Gnosticism in the early second century not only in Alexandria but in Middle Egypt as well, while Eusebius states[3] that in the persecution under Severus in A.D. 201 victims were brought for trial to Alexandria from all over Egypt, including the Thebaid—and they cannot all have been last-minute converts.

The Christian literary papyri may for convenience be divided into Biblical and other, even though in some cases the distinction may not have been as clear at the time they were written as it is now and though it is what they have in common that matters to our present argument. As evidence for our immediate purposes their limitations are obvious. None of them states explicitly where or when it was written; none carries the name of the scribe who wrote it; of very few has the title or colophon survived. Leaving on one side for the moment the information to be gleaned from the writing itself, we may observe that many of our texts have been found by excavation, and while this does not necessarily tell us where they were written, it does tell us where they were used. Some, however, were written on the verso of a roll already used for some documentary purpose and this provides us both with a provenance and an indication of date. Similarly, one of the earliest of our texts, the Baden fragment of Exodus and Deuteronomy, was dug up at Qarara in the Heracleopolite nome with a document in an identical hand wrapped round it,[4] while from a later period a

---

[1] See E. G. Turner, *GMAW*, and C. H. Roberts, *Greek Literary Hands* (Oxford, 1956); on the uncertainties of palaeographical dating see Turner, *Typology*, 2–4.

[2] P. Mich. 130 = H. 657.

[3] *H. E.* vi. 1.

[4] P. Baden iv, 56 = H. 33; for the document, see P. Baden iv, p. 24, which to the best of my knowledge has not been published. Qarara is on the site of the ancient Φυλακὴ ῾Ιππῶνος.

rough copy of the opening verses of Romans, perhaps a school exercise, was found tied up with a contract dated A.D. 316.[1]

If allowance is made for the fact that papyri are only found in the rain-free area of Egypt and that in consequence the whole of the Delta is *terra incognita*, the distribution of these texts is widely spread; sites where they have been found by scholarly excavation or to which there is good reason to attribute them are: in the Arsinoite nome the capital Arsinoe, Theadelphia, perhaps Socnopaiou Nesos;[2] Phylake Hipponos (Qarara); Oxyrhynchus; Antinoopolis; Hermopolis; Panopolis; Coptos; Thebes. Five of these sites—one in the Arsinoite not further identified, Qarara, Oxyrhynchus, Antinoopolis, and Coptos—have yielded texts datable to the second century. There is little reason to think that any of these texts were imported into Egypt with the possible exception of two categories: those written in languages other than Greek or Coptic, of which in our period there is only one, a Latin liturgical text of the late third or early fourth century,[3] and perhaps those written on parchment, which in Egypt, where papyrus was abundant and cheap, seems to have been little used before the fourth century, e.g. a third-century Genesis from Oxyrhynchus,[4] quite possibly Jewish, and a codex *de luxe* of Matthew and Luke of the first half of the fourth century from Hermopolis Magna.[5]

A characteristic of some of these texts is that they were found buried or said to have been found buried in jars, a practice which would explain why a number of them (only one, unfortunately, in the earliest group), if very rarely complete, yet are much more extensive than the great majority of secular

---

[1] P. Oxy. ii. 209 = H. 490.

[2] There is no firm evidence that any early Christian text came from this site. The great collection of papyri, Greek and demotic, in Vienna of undoubted Fayûmic provenance was not found by systematic excavation but was purchased as coming from Medinet (Arsinoe), Dimeh, and other sites in the Fayûm (see K. Preisendanz, *Papyrusfunde und Papyrusforschung* (Leipzig, 1933), p. 118). E. A. E. Reymond has convincingly argued that the demotic texts from the temple of Suchos derive not from Dimeh but from the large temple complex of Suchos near Arsinoe (M.P.E.R., N.S. ix, *A Medical Book from Crocodilopolis*, pp. 24–5). The same may hold of many of the Greek papyri; consequently (*pace* Preisendanz, op. cit. p. 236) the early Christian letter should be regarded as being of unknown or at best Fayûmic provenance, as should the early Psalter in Leipzig (= H. 224). It seems very probable that the site was abandoned before the end of the third century, though, as the evidence of some Coptic papyri suggests, it may have been reoccupied in the late fourth century (information from E. A. E. Reymond) and to this reoccupation some of the Byzantine Christian texts may be due. The Michigan excavators found no traces of Christianity on this site (see A. E. R. Boak), *Soknopaiou Nesos* (Ann Arbor, 1935), p. 21.

[3] P. Ryl. iii. 472 = H. 1211.

[4] P. Oxy. vii. 1007 = H. 5.

[5] P.S.I. i. 2+ii. 124 and P. Berol. 11863 = H. 356: see p. 12, n. 1.

manuscripts. To my knowledge, only one classical manuscript was discovered in a jar and that was included with an archive of family papers of the sixth century. To name only a few that are both relatively early and extensive, there are besides the Chester Beatty and Bodmer collections the Freer manuscripts in Washington and the Michigan *Shepherd* of Hermas. It was a Jewish habit both to preserve manuscripts by placing them in jars[2]—we may compare the instruction in *The Assumption of Moses*: 'To preserve the books which I have delivered unto thee thou shalt place them in an earthen vessel'[3]—and also to dispose of defective, worn-out, or heretical scriptures by burying them near a cemetery, not to preserve them but because anything that might contain the name of God might not be destroyed. The most celebrated case of such a burial of Jewish manuscripts, though by no means the only one, is that of the Dead Sea Scrolls and related finds in the wilderness of Judaea;[4] of Christian manuscripts a recent example, if outside our period, is the find of Gnostic codices at Nag Hammadi. It certainly looks as if this institution of a morgue for sacred but unwanted manuscripts was taken over from Judaism by the early Church. Carl Schmidt was told in 1934 that the Chester Beatty papyri had been found in a pitcher (much as some years later the Qumran scrolls were found) in the ruins of a church or monastery near Atfih (Aphroditopolis) and inferred both from their place of burial and from the fact that the papyri were already damaged when discovered that the Jewish practice was being followed.[5] Among other Christian manuscripts known to have been so buried are a fourth-century Psalter now in the British Library and a Coptic codex of the Fourth Gospel.[6]

[1] Some leaves of a manuscript of Menander were found at Kôm Ishgau (Aphroditopolis) together with an archive of private papers (see Preisendanz, *op. cit.* p. 113); but Dioscorus is hardly a guide to classical practice. Greek documents of the eighth century A.D. were discovered in a jar at Apollinopolis Magna (see E. G. Turner, *Greek Papyri*, p. 36).

[2] The placing of written material in jars for security was widespread throughout the ancient Near East: cf. R. de Vaux in *Revue Biblique* 56 (1949), pp. 591–2, J. T. Milik in *Biblica* 31 (1950), p. 504, and B. Couroyer in *Revue Biblique* 62 (1955), p. 76.

[3] R. H. Charles, *Apocrypha and Pseudepigrapha of the Old Testament* (Oxford, 1913), ii, p. 415; cf. also Jeremiah 32: 14.

[4] For the use of jars at Qumran see n. 2 above, and for the view that these discoveries came from the Genizah of the sect see Miller Burrows, *More Light on the Dead Sea Scrolls* (London, 1958), pp. 15 f. and 75–7. For the story in Eusebius (*H.E.* vi. 16) of the manuscript of the Psalter found by Origen near Jericho see P. Kahle, *The Cairo Genizah*[2], pp. 161 and 242.

[5] See *ZNTW* 30 (1931), p. 29 and *id.* 32 (1933), p. 225. As the area suggested is so close to the Fayûm the story finds some support in the presence of Coptic glosses in Old Fayûmic in the Isaiah codex.

[6] See P. E. Kahle, *Bala'izah* (London, 1954), p. 235, and H. Thompson, *The Gospel of John in Coptic* (Cambridge, 1932) and the same scholar's edition of the Coptic Acts and

If the hypothesis is accepted that Christians adopted the Jewish institution of a Genizah or depository for manuscripts, it would also explain why a collection such as the Chester Beatty or Bodmer includes manuscripts of differing date and, occasionally, more than one copy of the same book; they would have been deposited at different times and it would not be surprising if a volume relatively little used, such as Numbers and Deuteronomy, should be among the oldest. Manuscripts found in such circumstances would have been deposited by the community and so would constitute evidence for the history of the church in a way that private copies would not. And this attitude to the sacred text, common to Jews and Christians, explains the regular requisition and destruction of books by the authorities at times of persecution, so often recorded in the martyr acts.

A different case-history is provided by a codex of Philo, written in the later third century and found in a jar which had been walled up in a house at Coptos, i.e. not in or apparently near consecrated ground; it was preserved intact with its binding.[1] We may surmise that its owner concealed it with the intention of removing it from its hiding-place when danger had passed, either when Coptos was besieged and sacked by Diocletian in A.D. 292 or later in his reign during the last and severest of the persecutions. The codex is certainly Christian and not Jewish; among the scrap used to stuff the leather binding are small fragments of the first and substantial fragments of the third Gospel assigned to the later second century. Further, the editor of Philo has argued that the Coptos codex together with our medieval manuscripts derives from an archetype in Origen's library at Caesarea;[2] in that case we have evidence for the diffusion of scholarly texts in the provincial Church of Egypt.

We may next enquire whether the exterior characteristics of the texts suggests in any way their function or purpose. We have seen that in some cases the circumstances of the find point to community or church usage; but the majority of our papyri

---

Pauline Epistles published by the British School of Archaeology in Egypt (London, 1924). For a later period cf. the discoveries at Qasr Ibrim on the Nubian frontier (see J. M. Plumley in *JTS* 27 (1976), p. 34).

 [1] Paris, Bibl. Nat., Suppl. Gr. 1120 = H. 695. P. 4 (= H. 403) was used as stuffing for the binding: see C. H. Roberts, *Buried Books in Antiquity* (London, 1963), pp. 11–13. For the concealment of books in private houses in time of persecution cf. the martyrdom of Agape, Eirene and Chione (H. A. Musurillo, *The Acts of the Christian Martyrs* (Oxford, 1972), pp. 281 sq.) and Augustine, *Contra Cresc.* iii. 29. 33, iv. 56, 66.

 [2] *Philonis Opera* I, ed. L. Cohn–P. Wendland (Berlin, 1896), i, p. xlii.

were not found in jars but were rescued from the scrap-heaps and ruined houses of Graeco-Roman towns and villages and many, but not all of them, may have belonged to individual Christians. Among these, any texts written on the back of a roll or sheet discarded as waste declare themselves to be private copies, a view at times borne out by the manner of writing. One example is a Psalter written on the verso of a list of bank payments made in the years 143/4; unusual as it is for there to be a long gap between the writing on the recto and that on the verso, the Psalter is not likely to have been copied before the early third century.[1] Scrap paper was obviously suitable for a sermon such as we find in a London text written on the back of a document of A.D. 237[2] or for what appears to be, to judge from the hasty hand, a preacher's notes on a Florence papyrus.[3]

In the same category we might place one of the famous Oxyrhynchus 'Sayings of Jesus', now identified as part of the Gospel of Thomas;[4] this is on the verso of a land survey, while another Gnostic text of the third century is also written on the back of a document.[5] It must have been a scholarly Christian who used the margin of the famous letter of the mid-third century from a Christian in Rome to the community in Arsinoe for the first verses of Hebrews and then the back for the opening verses of Genesis both in the Septuagint version and in the literal Jewish version of Aquila.[6]

Such texts are not necessarily casual or occasional; private scholars might well prefer to use the cheapest material to hand. So on the back of a land register from Oxyrhynchus we find a Greek-Hebrew onomasticon, the interpretation in Greek of Hebrew names occurring in the New Testament;[7] it is dated to the third century and E. G. Turner has plausibly suggested that it may be part of a lost work of Origen—proof, if so, of the close and perhaps contemporary connection between the scholarly world of Alexandria and the provinces.

Not all texts written on improvised material need have been private. It may have been a paper shortage or just poverty that led one church to economize by sticking together sheets of papyrus already written on one side, fold them, and so form a

---

[1] P.S.I. viii. 921 = H. 174: on the date see H. I. Bell in *HTR* 37 (1944), p. 201.
[2] P. Lit. Lond. 228 = H. 1145. [3] P.S.I. vii. 758 = H. 1175.
[4] P. Oxy. iv. 654 = H. 593. [5] P. Oxy. i. 4 = H. 1070.
[6] P. Amh. i. 3 = H. 3 and 536.
[7] P. Oxy. xxxvi. 2745 = H. 1158; Turner's suggestion is made in the introduction to the ed. pr.

makeshift codex out of the unwritten sides; this was then used, about the year 300, to take a copy of Deuteronomy whose public character is strongly suggested by the addition of lectional aids—accents, breathings, punctuation, critical signs—to a carefully corrected text.[1]

More puzzling are cases where the verso of a roll carrying either a secular or a Christian text was reused for another literary work. The oddest perhaps is the roll from Oxyrhynchus which has on the recto a Latin epitome of Livy in a handsome uncial hand of the first half of the third century and on the verso the Epistle to the Hebrews for which the documents found with it suggest a late third century date.[2] Before Hebrews was copied the owner took care to patch the papyrus with scraps of third-century documents; it looks as if he was anxious to preserve both texts. A Christian in Middle Egypt competent in both Latin and Greek must have been something of a rarity. The roll is very much the exceptional format for any Biblical manuscript[3] and it is to be observed that the columns of Hebrews are numbered; while it is frequent enough for the pages of codices to be numbered I can think of hardly more than half-a-dozen instances of rolls with numbered columns;[4] it is a fair inference that the scribe was copying his text from a codex.

External characteristics of a different sort indicate a change in the Christian community towards the end of our period. The use of the codex goes back to the beginning of the Christian book; but for the first time towards the end of the third century we come across pocket codices, more often in parchment than in papyrus.[5] They are products of the book trade, often elegant and calligraphic to a degree; measuring from 15 × 11 cm.

[1] P. Ryl. i. 1 = H. 55.

[2] P. Oxy. iv. 657 (= H. 537) and 668. E. A. Lowe in *Codices Latini Antiquiores* ii[2] 208 assigns the Livy to the first half of the third century.

[3] Another papyrus in which a classical and a Christian text are found together is P. Lit. Lond. 207 with Psalms (= H. 109) on the recto and Isocrates *Ad Demonicum* on the verso. In both texts the syllables have been marked off to assist reading, and in the Psalms double letters within and between words are separated by an apostrophe (not always in the same hand). This and the frequent mistakes suggest that the texts were either written from memory or taken down none too intelligently from dictation. We may well get a glimpse here of a school where reading exercises were taken impartially from the scriptures and the classics.

[4] Other cases I have noted are: P.S.I. xii. 1284, P. Oxy. iii. 412, P: Ryl. III, 510, P. Mich. Inv. 6650 (*Wiener Studien* 79 (1966), pp. 190 sq.), P. Col. Inv. 437 (*Am. Journ. Phil.* 50 (1929), pp. 263–5, and the Marseilles Isocrates (*Mél. Graux* pp. 481 sq.). None is earlier than the later second century and most are later: possibly the influence of the codex is to be detected in all of them.

[5] On pocket codices see most recently E. G. Turner, *The Typology of the Early Codex*, pp. 25 and 29–30, and for the Mani codex, A. Henrichs and L. Koenen in *ZPE* 19 (1975) pp. 97 sq. Turner has established that pre-fourth-century parchment codices are invariably small in size and that the great parchment codices of the fourth century are modelled in point of format on the papyrus codex.

down to 7 × 5 cm.[1] they are far too small for public use; in some cases the number of lines to a page is as few as ten. One of them is surrounded with decorative lines,[2] another (of later date) has initial letters in red.[3] They are best regarded not as amulets but as devotional handbooks for the well-to-do, such as the ladies mentioned by Chrysostom who carried miniature texts of the Gospels round their necks.[4] (Their pagan counterparts were the miniature rolls of epigrams or love-poems written in elegant hands, designed to be easily carried and easily concealed.[5]) One, with only seventeen lines on its two pages amounting to three verses of Psalm 1 is written in so large a hand that it is tempting to think of it as meant for a child.[6]

The contents of these miniature books include edifying romances such as Tobit,[7] the Acts of John,[8] the Acts of Peter,[9] the story of Paul and Thecla from the *Acta Pauli*[10] and a section from *The Shepherd* of Hermas;[11] the Apocalypse[12] and 4 Esdras[13] may owe their place in this group to the popularity of apocalyptic in Egypt. Another, of the first half of the fourth century and running when complete to fifty-two pages, has a collection of texts in both Greek and Coptic, including passages from Daniel and Matthew.[14] The parchment booklets had their poorer relations on papyrus which do not set out to be

---

[1] Even smaller, though falling outside our period, is a late fourth century codex of Jonah (= H. 289) measuring 6 cm. in height and 5·5 cm. in breadth, with ten lines to a column and a range of letters to the line varying from six to four: see H. C. Youtie in *HTR* 38 (1945), pp. 195 ff. Smaller still is the Cologne Mani codex (see preceding note) of the fifth century; the page measures 4·5 cm. in height and 3·5 cm. in breadth while the area of writing is 3·5 × 2·5 cm. (= H. 1072).

[2] P. Oslo. Inv. 1661 (= H. 359), published by L. Amundsen in *Symbolae Osloenses* 24 (1945), pp. 121 ff., with a discussion of and references to other pocket codices, Greek and Coptic. The codex has extracts from Daniel and Matthew in Greek and Coptic.

[3] P. Oxy. v. 840 = H. 585, parchment, assigned to the fourth or fifth century; initial letters and punctuation marks are in red.

[4] *Hom.* 72, p. 703B: cited by L. Amundsen in *Christian Papyri from the Oslo Collection* (*Symbolae Osloenses* 24 (1945)), p. 140.

[5] For the pocket-sized rolls see W. Schubart, *Das Buch bei den Griechen u. Römern*² (Berlin, 1921), pp. 58 and 178.

[6] P. Oxy. xv. 1779 = H. 90.

[7] P. Oxy. xiii. 1594 = H. 82, parchment of the late third or early fourth century.

[8] P. Oxy. vi. 850 = H. 604, papyrus, fourth century.

[9] P. Oxy. vi. 849 = H. 603, parchment, third to fourth century.

[10] P. Ant. i. 13 = H. 610, parchment, fourth century. The skin is thin and translucent to an unusual degree and the script in its delicacy and regularity is reminiscent of that of the great biblical codices. Some of these parchment codices may have been imports into Egypt, brought by travellers or pilgrims at a time when Egypt was open to the outside world (and particularly the Christian world) as it had not been two centuries earlier.

[11] P. Oxy. xvii. 1783, parchment, early fourth century (= H. 659) and P. Oxy. xv. 1828, parchment, third century (= H. 665).

[12] P. Oxy. viii. 1080 = H. 561, parchment, fourth century.

[13] P. Oxy. vii. 1010 = H. 574, parchment, fourth century.

[14] See note 4 above.

expensive productions, but only ten on papyrus are known as against forty-five on parchment. The latter all carry works of Christian literature, as do all but one of the former, the exception being a technical work. On present evidence the miniature codex would seem to be a Christian invention.[1]

Apart from this last group, most of which belong to the fourth century rather than the third, our earliest Christian manuscripts are not for the most part products of the book trade, let alone *éditions de luxe*; most of them, we may suspect, are not private texts either in the usual sense. They have been best described as books privately published for a secret society.

If we examine the earliest group of Christian papyri with an eye to their graphic characteristics against other texts both literary and documentary, the latter including documents of a private as well as those of an official nature, some conclusions of interest result. By 'earliest' I mean those texts which in the general judgment of palaeographers are assigned to the second century,[2] though my list includes two, the first of the Oxyrhynchus Logia and the fragment of Irenaeus, dated by others to *c.* 200 or the early third century,[3] and omits two, the Bodmer St. John and the Chester Beatty codex of Ezekiel, Daniel and Esther which scholars of repute have placed firmly in the second century.[4] In the list that follows texts have been divided as a matter of convenience into Biblical and non-Biblical, even though the distinction, except for texts of the Old Testament, is anachronistic and might have surprised a reader of the second century; I have omitted one text that I have hitherto regarded as Christian but now consider more likely to be Jewish.[5] All the Biblical texts and two (11 and 13) of the non-Biblical are codices. With three exceptions, all to be dated towards the end

[1] Only one text of a canonical gospel or of part of one, apart from the Oslo codex (for which see p. 11, n. 1), has hitherto been found in this format: P.S.I. i. 2+ii. 124+P. Berol. Inv. 11863 (= H. 356), parchment, *c.* 300, found at Hermopolis, with extracts from Matthew and Luke. As a complete page measured 15 × 11 cm., it only just falls within the class of pocket codices.

[2] In the dating of early Christian papyri two contrary factors have to be borne in mind. In the belief that the introduction of the codex as an alternative to the roll was much later than it has since been proved to be, scholars of the calibre of Grenfell and Hunt sometimes went against their purely palaeographical judgment and so assigned too late a date to some early codices, both Christian and other (see the present writer in *JEA* 40 (1954), p. 94, with the references given in n. 4, and in *HTR* 46 (1953), p. 234). On the other hand and perhaps in reaction to the first factor, there is a tendency to claim an earlier date for some Christian texts, as E. G. Turner has noted (*Typology*, p. 4), than the facts warrant.

[3] See below, p. 14.

[4] Dates given for the Bodmer codex (p. 66) range from 'before A.D. 150' to early third century: see the references given under H. 326. For P. Chester Beatty ix see under H. 315.

[5] P. Oxy. iv. 656 = H. 12: see Appendix I.

of the century (nos. 8, 10, and 13), there is no calligraphic hand in the group.[1]

Biblical

1. P. Ryl. iii. 457 (= H. 462), St. John's Gospel.
2. P. Baden 4. 56 (= H. 33), Exodus, Deuteronomy.
3. P. Yale i. 1 (= H. 12), Genesis. The date assigned by the editor, C. B. Welles, 'perhaps between A.D. 80 and 100' was not backed by any detailed study of the writing and has not found acceptance. I can find no parallel to the shape of *mu* (M) in this papyrus earlier than the later second century (P. Oxy. i. 26; also reproduced in W. Schubart, *Griechische Paläographie*, Abb. 83) and would be reluctant to date the papyrus before the middle of the century.
4. P. Chester Beatty vi (= H. 52), Numbers, Deuteronomy. On the date of this codex, see Appendix II.
5. P. Ant. i. 7 (= H. 179), Psalms.
6. P. Lips. 170 (= H. 224), Psalms.
7. Bodl. MS. Gr. bibl. g. 5 (P) (= H. 151), Psalms.
8. P. Barc. Inv. 1+P. Magdalen College, Oxford Gr. 18+P. Paris, Bibl. Nat. Suppl. Gr. 1120 (= H. 336 and 403), St. Matthew, St. Luke. There can in my opinion be no doubt that all these fragments come from the same codex which was reused as packing for the binding of the late third century codex of Philo (= H. 695). An apparent discrepancy was that Ἰησοῦς appeared as ιϲ in the Paris fragments and as ιη in the Oxford fragments; the correct reading in the latter, however, is ιϲ, as can be checked in the photograph.[2]
9. P. Ryl. i. 5 (= H. 534), Titus. To the opinions cited by van Haelst should be added that of H. I. Bell, 'definitely second century'.[3]
10. P. Oxy. xxxiv. 2683 (= H. 372), St. Matthew.

Non-Biblical[4]

11. P. Lond. Christ. 1 (= H. 586), the Egerton Gospel.[5]

[1] For references to the first and subsequent publications and to discussions of dating the reader is referred to van Haelst's *Catalogue*; comments are only made here if there are additional views or evidence to be taken into account. Attention should also be drawn to the dating of codices in E. G. Turner's *Typology* where later dates are favoured for some of those discussed here.

In an article in *JTS* 50 (1949), p. 157 I placed both P. Chester Beatty ix (= H. 315) and viii in the second century, if on the borderline; for both I should now prefer the description 'c. 200', though the distinction is a fine one.

[2] For the date, on which palaeographers are agreed, see the introduction to the Oxford fragments in *HTR* 46 (1953), pp. 233 ff.

[3] In *HTR* 37 (1944), p. 201.

[4] On P. Fay. 2, the so-called 'Psalm of the Naassenes', often classified as a Christian text (= H. 1066), see Appendix III.

[5] To the bibliography in van Haelst *Catalogue* add G. Mayeda, *Das Leben-Jesu-Fragment Papyrus Egerton 2 und seine Stellung in der urchristlichen Literaturgeschichte* (Berne, 1946).

12. P. Mich. 130 (= H. 657), a fragment of *The Shepherd* of Hermas, written on the verso of a roll carrying a documentary text of the third quarter of the second century.

13. P. Oxy. i. 1 (= H. 594), Logia, now identified as part of the Gospel of Thomas.[1]

14. P. Oxy. iii. 405 (= H. 671), Irenaeus, *Adversus Haereses*.[2]

The first editors of these papyri, if we except the three noted above as calligraphic, are apt to describe the hands as 'informal uncial' (*uncial* by itself meaning little more than that the writing was not a normal cursive and was intended to be easily read) or as belonging to 'the plain style'. What I think they all, in varying degrees, have in common is that, though the writing is far from unskilled, they are the work of men not trained in calligraphy and so not accustomed to writing books, though they were familiar with them; they employ what is basically a documentary hand but at the same time they are aware that it is a book, not a document on which they are engaged. They are not personal or private hands; in most a degree of regularity and of clarity is aimed at and achieved. Such hands might be described as 'reformed documentary'. (One advantage for the palaeographer in such hands is that with their close links to the documents they are somewhat less difficult to date than purely calligraphic hands.) They range from the straight, carefully written documentary hand of the Baden Exodus and Deuteronomy to the Egerton Gospel and the Rylands Titus which declare themselves to be books but which in their use of ligature and in certain letter forms betray their documentary affinities. In between come the Rylands St. John[3] and the Chester Beatty Numbers and Deuteronomy which might be described as quasi-literary; the scribe of the latter does indeed employ certain literary devices such as spacing, iota adscript, and paragraph marks, but he does so irregularly

---

[1] On this H. I. Bell wrote (*loc. cit.*, p. 202) '. . . dated by Grenfell and Hunt themselves second or third century, and I do not think the earlier date is at all unlikely'. When it was first published (*ΛΟΓΙΑ ΙΗΣΟΥ*, London 1897) the comparative material available to Grenfell and Hunt for dating was relatively small. It is worth quoting their opinion at this date: 'The general probabilities of the case, the presence of the usual contractions found in biblical MSS, and the fact that the papyrus was in book, not roll form, put the first century out of the question. The date therefore probably falls within the period 150–300 A.D., though that cannot be said with any approach to certainty. Any attempt to distinguish between second and third century uncials is, in the present paucity of dated material, extremely precarious.' In *New Sayings of Jesus* (London, 1904, p. 9) they ascribed it without further discussion to the third century.

[2] In their edition of the fragment before its identity was established, Grenfell and Hunt commented that the hand 'is not later than the first half of the third century and might be as old as the latter part of the second'.

[3] The scribe's natural style is revealed in the formation of the looped alpha and the upsilon.

and is clearly not at home with them[1] with the result that he falls between two stools.[2] In all of them there is a family resemblance; in none can be traced the work of the professional calligrapher or the rapid, informal hand of the private scholar.[3] Works of secular literature are also written in such hands, but there is not the same preponderance of them.

To judge from their hands, ⌈the earliest Christian books were essentially books for use, not, as Jewish Rolls of the Law sometimes were, almost cult objects;⌋that was only possible for a publicly recognized and protected cult so that the Christian equivalent is not found before the great codices of the fourth century. Some other habits of the writers of these texts point in the same direction. A documentary practice, if sometimes an unconscious one,⌐ is that of leaving spaces between words or more often groups of words, for example in contracts,[4] in contrast with the strict literary principle of *scriptio continua* with breaks only at the end of sections; this can be found in some early Christian texts.⌋An engaging example of the way in which a scribe betrays his background can be seen in the early fourth century codex—the use of 'reformed documentary' continues well into the fourth century[5]—that contains Melito's treatise on the Passion. When he had to write the word χαίρειν,

---

[1] He is irregular in his use of *nu ἐφελκυστικόν* and there are examples of wrong word-division at fol. 102, col. i, l. 4 σκην|ην and at fol. 103ᵛ, col. i. l. 4 διαβ|αινοντα. Most of his mistakes were corrected by a second hand.

[2] Similarly the scribe of no. 6 employs iota adscript as well as accents, breathings and other reading-marks; but the hand itself betrays strong documentary influence, e.g. the *mu* with tail to the left and the *xi*. Some of these early O.T. texts may have been copied from better written Jewish manuscripts in which such literary practices as the use of iota adscript would have been usual. A later example of the use of iota adscript in a professional semi-cursive is the Freer Minor Prophets (= H. 284) of c. 300.

[3] This type of hand (for which see E. G. Turner, *Scribes and Scholars of Oxyrhynchus* in M.P.E.R., N.S. 5, p. 144) is found in Christian texts of the next century, e.g. in P. Iand. v, 69 = H. 648 (? Origen).

[4] Also in official and administrative documents such as the Gnomon of the Idios Logos (B.G.U. v: plate in W. Schubart, *Griechische Paläographie*, Abb. 36).

[5] Some examples are:

(a) P. Oxy. ii. 208+xv. 1781 = H. 428, a third-century codex of St. John's Gospel, written in an 'informal semi-literary' hand.

(b) P. Mich. 129 = H. 660, a third-century codex of *The Shepherd* of Hermas, the scribe of which is described by the editor as 'accomplished but accomplished in letter writing'.

(c) P. Mich. Inv. 6652 = H. 380, a third-century codex of St. Matthew written in a regular, fluent, highly compressed documentary hand with cursive forms; as the reading marks indicate, a utility codex for public reading.

(d) P. Mich. III 137 = H. 378, another papyrus codex of the First Gospel of the later third or early fourth century with a very crowded page and only distinguished from a document by the *nomina sacra*.

(e) The Berlin Genesis = H. 4, a papyrus codex, irregular in layout and design, and written in an unadulterated cursive: in spite of some accents and apostrophes, probably a private and unprofessional work, to be dated between A.D. 270 and 320.

(f) P. Oxy. vi. 850 = H. 604, an early fourth-century codex of the Acts of John, written in an 'irregular, rather inelegant' hand.

to rejoice, he was so familiar with its usage, *greeting*, in the preamble to letters that unreflectingly he left a space each side of the word as though it had been preceded by the name of an addressee—something no professional copyist of books would ever do.[1] I can think of no similar slip in any papyrus of classical literature.

There is another documentary practice taken over by the scribes of Christian manuscripts that became of some importance in the development of writing. In documents the first word of the text, and in letters the name of the addressee as well, often carries an enlarged initial letter, as does the beginning of a new clause or section; this can be traced back to the second century B.C.[2] Two clear examples in our period are the official document known as the Gnomon of the Idios Logos (the Rule Book of the Special Account) from the middle of the second century A.D. and P. Brem. 5 (*c.* A.D. 117), a document written in the chancery of the Epistrategus. This practice is quite alien to the literary papyri of the Ptolemaic and Roman periods;[3] but it is found, when the texts are not so fragmentary that there is no evidence, in the early Christian papyri. Thus in the Egerton Gospel there is a tendency to enlarge the letter following a pause and also the first letter on a page, even though it does not stand at the beginning of a sentence;[4] at the same time the first letter of each line is often slightly enlarged, as it is in the Chester Beatty Numbers and Deuteronomy.[5]

Here may lie the solution of a problem in European

(*g*) P. Chester Beatty v = H. 7, a papyrus codex of Genesis of the later third century, whose hand is not so much that of a letter writer as of a chancery clerk.

(*h*) The Freer Minor Prophets = H. 284, a papyrus codex of the later third century.

(*i*) P. Yale Inv. 415 = H. 522, a papyrus codex of Ephesians of the third century.

[1] P. Chester Beatty xii, with pl. ii; for this codex which contained as well as Melito on the Passion the last chapters of Enoch and Pseudo-Ezekiel see H. 578, 579, and 677. In his edition Campbell Bonner remarked (p. 14) that while it was unmistakably not a document there was 'no literary hand . . . closely resembling it'.

Documentary influence on literary texts is by no means of one kind; while this manuscript reflects the style of the professional letter-writer, P. Chester Beatty v (= H. 7) recalls the official Chancery style of the period.

[2] Cf. p. 15, n. 1 and see also B.M. Pap. 1527, an honorary decree written between A.D. 138 and 160, reproduced in Turner, *GMAW*, no. 69. Such enlargement is, naturally enough, most conspicuous in the first letter of the dating formula, cf. Schubart, op. cit., Abb. 37.

[3] An exception that proves the rule is the occasional use of this practice in the *Acts of the Pagan Martyrs*; as already noted (see above, p. 3), these sub-literary texts have something in common with Christian papyri.

[4] See P. Lond. Christ. i, l. 82. Other good examples are the Chester Beatty Melito (see n. 1 above) and the parchment codex of 2 John from Antinoe = H. 555; in the latter the initial letter of a new section, even in the middle of a line, is similarly enlarged (cf. plate in ed. pr.).

[5] The tendency found in both manuscripts for the writing to grow smaller towards the end of the line is a documentary habit not unknown to the literary papyri, cf. e.g. P. Lit. Lond. 132 (Hyperides).

palaeography. Wilhelm Schubart concluded[1] that in this respect there was no connection between the early Greek documents on the one hand and the calligraphic Christian manuscripts of the fourth century and later and medieval manuscripts in general on the other hand; but the connecting link is, I think, clearly to be discerned in the early Christian papyri with their documentary background.

Writing as a Latin palaeographer, E. A. Lowe came to the conclusion that the practice was very ancient and therefore pagan in origin;[2] but in fact it is not to be found in our earliest manuscripts of the Latin classics from Egypt, but does occur in the fragments of the Old Latin Genesis from Oxyrhynchus, dated to the fourth century,[3] while in the roughly contemporary codex of Cyprian (not of Egyptian provenance) the first letter of a new chapter or section is conspicuously enlarged.[4] In this, as in other respects, Latin palaeography follows in the wake of Greek. In the Codex Alexandrinus the first letter of the first complete line of each new section or paragraph is enlarged; in a fourth-century Psalter from the Fayûm, now in Berlin,[5] the initial letter of each verse is twice the usual size.[6] And a forerunner of the ornamental initial letter may be descried in a leaf of an uncanonical Gospel from Oxyrhynchus written on parchment in the late fourth or early fifth century in which the initial letter of each sentence is both enlarged and written in red.[7]

At times, in imitation again of documentary practice,[8] an initial letter is not only enlarged but also extruded into the margin; thus in the Chester Beatty Ezekiel[9] of the early third century the beginning of a new section or the first complete line of a new section is marked in this way, while in the

---

[1] Op. cit., pp. 173-4.

[2] See his *Palaeographical Papers* (Oxford, 1972), i, pp. 196 ff.

[3] P. Oxy. viii. 1073 = H. 1202; in a contemporary legal fragment, P. Ant. i. 22, the first letter of each page, even when in the middle of a word, is enlarged.

[4] *Cod. Lat. Ant.* iv. 458: cf. also J. Mallon, *Paléographie Romaine* (Madrid, 1952), pl. xxx, no. 5.

[5] BKT. viii = H. 142.

[6] In the earliest Latin Christian text, P. Ryl. iii. 472 = H. 1211, an enlarged letter is not used either for the beginning of a new section in the middle of a line or for the first letter of a page.

[7] P. Oxy. v. 840 = H. 585. Red ink is used to pick out the abbreviation πετ for Πέτρος in the so-called Fayûm Gospel (actually from Heracleopolis) of the third century (P. Vindob. Graec. G. 2325 = H. 589) and occasionally to overline the *nomina sacra* in a fifth-century Coptic codex of the Pauline Epistles (see P. E. Kahle, *Bala'izah*, p. 351).

[8] Cf. Schubart, op. cit., Abb. 37 and 39 (both of the second century).

[9] = H. 315. Some other Christian texts with this feature are P. Oxy. ix. 1169 = H. 344, (St. Matthew), P. Oxy. xi. 1351 = H. 50 (Leviticus), P. Berol. 6747 = H. 142 (Psalter), and P. Oxy. xvii. 2068 (liturgy: possibly Jewish, see Appendix I).

second-century Luke[1] no. 8 above) the letter projects but is not enlarged. In secular literary texts this practice, essentially documentary, is confined in the Roman period to commentaries and lists.[2]

Documentary practice may not have been the only influence on Christian scribes. In the manuscript of the Minor Prophets found in a cave near Engedi in Judaea and dated between 50 B.C. and A.D. 50,[3] an enlarged letter, preceded by a small blank space, marks the beginning of a new phrase, while verses are marked off by larger spaces. This may well have been standard Hebrew usage in texts such as this, clearly intended for liturgical reading.

Equally significant of the independence of Christian manuscripts of the secular tradition is the practice to which E. G. Turner has drawn attention of writing cardinal numbers in symbols, not in words. He writes,[4] 'I know of only one Greek book MS. (an unpublished papyrus of Strabo) in which figures are not written out in full, but given in numerical notation; but the use of numerical notation and of abbreviations of this kind is common in documentary papyri and is found in copies of the sacred scriptures'. In only four of our earliest texts,[5] which are mainly small and fragmentary, do numbers occur; but in three cases symbols are used and in the fourth must be presumed on grounds of space to have been used. The practice is not invariable and on occasion both systems are used in the same manuscript,[6] particularly where lower numbers are involved; but once established it persisted. It is found, for example, in the Vaticanus and Sinaiticus and in later codices; such manuscripts are not all of Egyptian provenance, and this suggests that our earliest papyri may be representative of early Christian books in general. Whether in this and in more important respects there was some authoritative production that set the standard, we do not know and are not likely to know.

[1] See p. 13 above; the same practice is to be seen in the Bodmer St. John = H. 426.

[2] Cf. Turner, *GMAW*, p. 9. In the Livy Epitome (P. Oxy. iv. 668) each entry begins with the name of the consul of the year; the initial letter projects but is not enlarged.

[3] = H. 285: see E. J. Revell, *Bulletin of the John Rylands Library* 54 (1971), pp. 214 ff. In an article in *Stud. Pap.* xv (1976), pp. 131 ff. the same writer has observed that the system of paragraphing in this parchment roll, as also in the contemporary P. Fouad 266 (= H. 56), is very close to that of the Hebrew Masoretic text, both the paragraphing by initial space and initial letter and that by punctuation (in the second hand). This might indicate that the method of paragraphing by the initial letter was of Jewish origin.

[4] *GMAW*, p. 18.

[5] Nos. 3, 4, 8, 13 in the list above, pp. 13–14.

[6] e.g. in the Bodmer St. John; here the scribe with the eccentricity that characterizes him uses both systems, cf. 5. 5 with 6. 10 or 8. 57. In the Bodmer Luke/John codex (= H. 406) only the thousands are written out while δύο and τρεῖς are expressed in symbols.

It has not, I think, been observed that this practice is confined to Christian literary manuscripts and is not found in Jewish manuscripts of the Greek version of the Old Testament. In the extensive roll of Genesis and Deuteronomy in Cairo,[1] certainly of pre-Christian date, in the Qumran Leviticus,[2] and in the roll of the Minor Prophets from Engedi,[3] numbers are regularly written out.

In the earliest manuscripts, but not, as far as my observation goes, in later ones, other abbreviations familiar from documents are occasionally found. Thus, when the scribe of the Chester Beatty Numbers and Deuteronomy was faced with writing at Numbers 31: 24 the Greek for 'ruler of an hundred', his mind and his pen immediately went back to the Greek for *centurio* written with a χ (representing the -$\alpha\rho\chi\eta s$ termination) and a superscript ρ ($= 100$).

There are two stigmata of Christian texts, the most conspicuous and the most important, that I have not mentioned; the early and consistent use of the codex and the *nomina sacra*. The first has been amply discussed elsewhere;[4] the historical and theological significance of the second will be discussed in the next chapter.

We have noted one point in which Christian manuscripts may resemble Jewish, another in which they certainly differ; on the whole the differences are more striking than the resemblances. Our evidence for Graeco-Jewish manuscripts of the Greek period is scanty, but it is remarkably consistent. These manuscripts, whether from Palestine or from Egypt, are outstanding for the elegance and the regularity of their writing. To look at the roll of the Minor Prophets from Engedi, the Deuteronomy fragment of the second century B.C. in the Rylands collection together with the Fouad roll of Genesis and Deuteronomy in Cairo is to wonder whether there was not a definite and consciously adopted style for the writing of the Law in Greek that persisted for two centuries and probably longer.[5] The contrast between the hieratic elegance of the Graeco-Jewish rolls of the Law and the workaday appearance of the first Christian codices (whether of the Old Testament or of

---

[1] P. Fouad Inv. 266. In the still earlier Rylands Deuteronomy fragment (= H. 57) there is no instance of a numeral.

[2] = H. 49.

[3] = H. 285.

[4] A second edition of my British Academy paper on the codex (prepared by T. C. Skeat and myself) will be published shortly.

[5] See Appendix I for a list of Old Testament and other Jewish literary texts of the Roman period and for the criteria to be applied in distinguishing them from Christian manuscripts.

Christian writings) is less remarkable when we remember how exposed and precarious were the possessions and especially the books of a sect under suspicion and liable to intermittent persecution and that the specifically Christian writings, whether Gospels or collections of the sayings of the Lord, laid no claim to inspiration; the only book of the New Testament that explicitly makes the claim is the Apocalypse of St. John, the last book to be admitted, and that reluctantly, to the Canon by the Eastern Church.

This last point should not be pressed; reverence for a sacred text need not be, though it often is, closely allied to format or script. It is generally accepted that the first scriptures (in the strict sense) of the early church were the books of the Old Testament and that in the transmission of the Christian message the oral tradition took precedence over the written word; hence it is not at all surprising that some of our earliest Christian manuscripts should be of the Old Testament. What is surprising is that the format in which they are written should be the codex and not the roll; this startling break with Jewish tradition implies, I think, that these early manuscripts of the Old Testament had been preceded by specifically Christian works with which the new format originated. For this to happen, these writings must have exercised some degree of authority, a point that must have been reached before the end of the first century. (The question of authority and its source is discussed in the next chapter in connection with the *nomina sacra*.) As for elegance of script, the early communities may well not have had access to the services of skilled scribes such as the synagogue could command. Philo observes[1] that the scriptures should not be copied by scribes working for money, but by students of the Law; translated into Christian terms this would mean that in their production economic and social factors as well as religious were at work and that the business-like hand of the early texts mirrors the character and circumstances of the communities that used them.

From this survey of the externals of our earliest Christian manuscripts we can conclude that their writing is based, with some changes and with a few exceptions, on the model of the documents, not on that of Greek classical manuscripts nor on that of the Greco-Jewish tradition. It antedates, as does the system of *nomina sacra*, the emergence in the later second century of the Catechetical School of Alexandria as a powerful influence

[1] *De. spec. leg.* iv, 163.

throughout and beyond Egypt, and was sufficiently well-established for certain of its practices to persist in manuscripts of the following centuries of quite another character. Behind this group of papyri it is not difficult to envisage the men familiar to us from the documentary papyri in the Arsinoite or Oxyrhynchus: tradesmen, farmers, minor government officials to whom knowledge of and writing in Greek was an essential skill, but who had few or no literary interests. Even if of Jewish race, they would not know Hebrew, a rare accomplishment among the Jews of Egypt in the first century and a half of Roman rule;[1] not only do we not find the Hebrew name of God transcribed in Christian texts, but the scribes sometimes had trouble with Hebrew names, witness a passage in the Chester Beatty papyrus of Deuteronomy where the Hebrew name Σανειρ is transformed into Greek ἀνήρ.[2] I do not find it so easy to see in the writers of these early papyri Gnostic intellectuals, as the theories of some scholars would demand.

But if the style is documentary in origin, it is documentary with a difference. Several of the early texts carry reading aids—accents, breathings, punctuation, marks to indicate foreign words; the most purely documentary in script, the Baden Exodus–Deuteronomy, uses a wedge-shaped line-filler to round off a line.[3] All this is quite alien to the documents[4] and not all that common in the literary papyri, not at least in the abundance in which they are found in some Christian texts. The scribe of the third century codex of *The Shepherd* of Hermas in Michigan[5] not only is lavish in the use of reading aids, but at times added marginal notes and corrections; he seems to have been working from two copies. The makeshift codex of Deuteronomy of the early fourth century referred to above[6] is crudely written but is equipped with critical signs and is a careful

---

[1] See V. A. Tcherikover in his Prolegomena to *CPJ* i, pp. 30–2, 44, 93 ff., 101–2 and 107–8. Whether Philo himself knew any Hebrew is a matter of debate; Hebrew did not revive in Egypt till after the disastrous war of A.D. 133 when the surviving Jews tended to turn their backs on Greek civilization.

[2] At Deut. 4. 10; the correction was made by the second hand.

[3] I know of no example of this practice (for which see *GMAW*, p. 6) in a document.

[4] A rare, if not unique, exception to the rule that no document is ever accented is P. Ryl. iv. 624, a self-conscious 'literary' letter written by his son to a high official who was a member of a cultured pagan revivalist group in Hermopolis in the early fourth century. To the references given on p. 114 to the very occasional lectional aids to be found in documents should be added P. Herm. Rees 2, 5, and 6, all letters belonging to the same group as the Rylands letter and two of them to the same addressee, and P. Ross-Georg. ii, 43 (a rough breathing). On the Rylands letter and related documents see now A. Moscadi in *Aegyptus* 50 (1970), pp. 88 ff.

[5] = H. 657.

[6] See p. 10 above. In his publication of his text A. S. Hunt remarked on the 'surprising frequency' of accents and breathings.

text. In the second century, locally produced texts such as the scrap of *The Shepherd* on the back of a document from the Fayûm or the Baden Exodus–Deuteronomy might be carefully collated and corrected; the numerous duplications and omissions of the first hand of the Chester Beatty Numbers–Deuteronomy codex were put right by a corrector. This scrupulous reproduction of the text may be a legacy from Judaism and reminds us that no more in this period than in any other does quality of book production go hand in hand with quality of text.

The frequent employment of lectional aids points to a conclusion already reached on other grounds, that most of these texts were intended for church use,[1] to be read in public. A telling example is the scrap of *The Shepherd*, mentioned above, whose scribe uses an all-purpose *siglum* to indicate accents or breathings, no doubt a much-needed aid in the most inelegantly written of our early texts. (*The Shepherd* was widely regarded as scripture at this time and remained a candidate for canonization; it was especially used for the instruction of catechumens.[2] Its popularity in provincial Egypt may give us a better insight into the character of the churches than anything else.)

One other reflection is prompted by some of these manuscripts—the Egerton Gospel, the Luke from Coptos, or the Chester Beatty Numbers–Deuteronomy—that the communities which owned them, while not rich, were not conspicuously poor.

It was remarked above that among the second-century Christian texts were a few whose style of writing did not tally with that of the majority. While we have to remember that there is no hard and fast distinction between the 'reformed documentary' and the more relaxed literary styles,[3] there are three[4]

---

[1] In the Chester Beatty Numbers and Deuteronomy at fol. 65 verso a coronis is inserted, apparently to mark the end of a passage set for reading. Other such markings are to be found in P. Chester Beatty ix and P. Mich. iii. 137.

The scribe of P. Chester Beatty vi, together with his frequent itacisms, occasionally inserts an iota adscript, also found in P. Chester Beatty v (= H. 7), P. Rein. ii. 5 (= H. 43), both of the third century and in the Freer Minor Prophets.

[2] On the use of *The Shepherd* for the instruction of catechumens see Tertullian, *de Pud.* 10. 39.

[3] Two of the three Psalters, nos. 5 and 7, may in this respect be regarded as marginal. Both are handsome and carefully written texts, and though n. 5 has some ligatures and other traces of cursive influence, e.g. the shape of iota, parallels to it can be found in Greek literary papyri. The editors of the Bodleian fragment, no. 7, while finding earlier examples of the style in the Rylands St. John and in a document of A.D. 94 (P. Fay. 110), align it with no. 5 and less surely with P. Oxy. iv. 656 and viii. 1074 (for which see Appendix I). The closest

[Note 3 continued and note 4 opposite

papyri whose different character is plainly marked. One, no. 14 in the list, certainly comes from the later part of the century and on palaeographical grounds the other two, nos. 8 and 10, may be ascribed to the same period. These are incontrovertibly literary in style. In the first, no. 8, the text is divided into sections on a system also found in the Bodmer codex of Luke and John[1] that recurs in some of the great fourth-century codices and was clearly not personal to this scribe. Once again we find in a manuscript of this early period a characteristic that appears to be not specifically Egyptian but of wider application. In its handsome script as well as in its organization—there are three different positions for punctuation as well as omission and quotation signs—it is a thoroughgoing literary production.[2]

In this respect it keeps company with no. 14, a fragment of a roll from Oxyrhynchus of which Grenfell and Hunt wrote in 1903 that it was 'not later than the first half of the third century and might be as old as the later part of the second'—where I should place it. It was subsequently identified as belonging to the *Adversus Haereses* of Irenaeus, written in Lyons about A.D. 180. (We may observe that the conventional format of the roll was often retained for works of Christian scholarship when the codex was almost always used for texts of the Bible.) The significance of the presence of this text in Oxyrhynchus, which is written in a handsome professional hand, will be discussed later. The third, again from Oxyrhynchus, is part of a leaf of a codex of Matthew in an elegant hand assigned by the editors to the late second century; it also has what was or became a standard system of chapter division as well as punctuation and breathings.

In his *Scribes and Scholars of Oxyrhynchus*[3] E. G. Turner has identified among the city's residents some well-known scholars—among them Pollux—who maintained their association with Alexandria, some being professors at the Museum, and to whom or to whose interest some of our classical texts from that site are in all probability to be ascribed. One of the criteria Turner

---

parallels, however, that I can find to this hand are two documents, P. Merton ii. 73 of A.D. 160–3, and P. Aberd. 174 of A.D. 154–9. While neither of these two Psalters would be mistaken at first glance for a document, both stand in the general tradition of early Christian palaeography.

[4] P. Oxy. iv. 656 (for which see Appendix I), if regarded as Christian rather than Jewish, would make a fourth.

[1] See the introduction to P. Bodmer xiv by R. Kasser, pp. 14 ff., who points out that a very similar system is employed in the Bodmer St. John.

[2] None the less, the practice of writing ordinal numbers in symbols is maintained.

[3] Cf. p. 15 n. 3.

employs for identifying the 'scholarly' texts is the presence of critical signs and other scribal practices; it is tempting to posit a similar connection between the few professional Christian texts, i.e. those with critical signs or other scholarly apparatus as distinct from reading aids, and the Catechetical School of Alexandria. The School first attracts attention towards the end of the second century, but Eusebius implies[1] that it went back well behind Pantaenus who was in charge of it before A.D. 180.[2] And in his Schweich Lectures for 1946[3] G. Zuntz has convincingly argued that the Corpus Paulinum was produced by the methods of Alexandrian scholarship and possibly in Alexandria at the beginning of the century. 'The conclusion is almost inescapable', he writes, 'that already in the latter half of the second century the Alexandrian bishopric possessed a scriptorium which by its output set the standard for the Alexandrian type of Biblical manuscripts'.[4] In that case it is not a matter for surprise if scholarly manuscripts from Alexandria penetrated provincial Egypt and there is nothing inherently implausible in the presence in Oxyrhynchus of a copy of a book written by Irenaeus about A.D. 180. Whether there was a scriptorium for Christian books at Oxyrhynchus, now or in the third century, as Turner has given reason to think there was for secular learning, is unknown, but the large number of Christian texts from the site makes it not unlikely.[5]

The connection between Christian Alexandria and provincial Egypt is plain to see in the next century. From an unknown site we have a codex of the homilies of Origen contemporary with the writer or very little later,[6] while another text of the first half of the third century[7] has been ascribed to him by Dr. Chadwick, as have two others later in the century, one from Oxyrhynchus,[8] the other from Hermopolis,[9] all in literary hands

---

[1] *H.E.* v. 10. 1.

[2] L. Alfonsi in *Aegyptus* 56 (1976), pp. 101 ff. argues on the basis of a documentary analogy that Pantaenus was the head of a private school, not that of the Church, but I do not find his argument convincing.

[3] *The Text of the Epistles* (London, 1953), pp. 271 sq. and especially p. 275 where he makes the case for the existence of a full critical text, perhaps originating in Alexandria c. A.D. 100; see below p. 54. On the early history of the School see Eusebius, *H.E.* v, 10. I.

[4] That it existed earlier is likely; see below, p. 54.

[5] That Oxyrhynchus in the third century may have been something of a Christian intellectual centre is suggested by the presence there of an autograph manuscript of an anti-Jewish dialogue (P. Oxy. xvii. 2070 = H. 1154).

[6] P. Bonn. i. 1 = H. 688.

[7] P. Lond. Christ. 2 = H. 691; the editors date the hand to 'well before 250'.

[8] P. Oxy. ii. 406 = H. 1152; for the ascription to Origen see P. G. Ausenda in *Aegyptus*, 20 (1940), pp. 43 ff.

[9] P. Giss. Univ. Bibl. 2. 17 = H. 694.

with the exception of the last. This may be placed in the category of private scholarly hands identified as such among secular texts by Turner by the fluency of the writing (often close to cursive), the frequent use of abbreviations, and the presence of critical signs.[1]

The origin and development of the Church in Egypt to which not only the form but the content of some of the early papyri will contribute is a matter for later consideration; meanwhile from this survey of their exterior characteristics a provisional picture may be drawn. To start with, we note that texts mainly but not exclusively of the canonical books are widely dispersed in Middle and Upper Egypt; many come from Oxyrhynchus, but we have no reason to think that at this time the Church in Oxyrhynchus was stronger than it was elsewhere. This points to the careful and regular use of the scriptures by the local communities. They themselves, if we can faintly discern them mirrored in their books, would seem to have been composed not so much of the intellectuals or the wealthy as of ordinary men of the middle or lower middle classes. (Conditions may well have been different in Alexandria as they were in the provinces in the later third century.) Towards the end of the century the impact of the new scholarship begins to make itself felt; those few manuscripts suggest a higher standard in both economic and cultural terms. Jewish influences —as well as divergences from Jewish practice—can be traced here and there, though the evidence for a strongly Jewish form of Christianity has still to be presented, and in two manuscripts there is more than a hint of Gnostic activity; but the picture is less sensational than has sometimes been suggested.

[1] In this connection attention should be drawn to P. Grenf. i. 5, a leaf from a papyrus codex of Ezekiel (= H. 314), of the late third or early fourth century that carries Origen's hexaplaric sigla.

II

NOMINA SACRA: ORIGINS AND SIGNIFICANCE

NOMINA SACRA[1] as a term in Greek and Latin palaeography denotes a strictly limited number of words, at most fifteen, the sacral character of which, intrinsic or contextual, is emphasized by abbreviating the word in question, normally by contraction, occasionally in the earliest period by suspension. A horizontal line is placed above the abbreviation as a warning that the word cannot be pronounced as written, as it was in documents with numerals, and where, as is usual, contraction is used, the treatment of the end of the word is governed by strict rules. The subject as a tool for palaeographers was invented by Ludwig Traube, to whom the name itself is due, in a fundamental monograph published nearly seventy years ago. Some of his conclusions can now be seen to be erroneous, thanks largely to discoveries made since he wrote; he was in any case more concerned with palaeography and less with the historical questions which are our business. Though there are earlier references to the method of writing the Tetragrammaton and to the monograms for Ἰησοῦς and Χριστός, no ancient author alludes to the system—familiar to anyone who has ever looked at a Biblical manuscript or indeed at a Christian Greek or Latin inscription of any period—before Christian of Stavelot in the ninth century;[2] that they should thus be taken for granted is an indication of their antiquity.

The purpose of the system was demonstrably not to save either space or the scribe's time; a free space is often left round the abbreviation and the time saved by writing a four-letter

[1] The principal discussions of the subject to date are:

L. Traube, *Nomina Sacra* (Munich, 1906).

A. H. R. E. Paap, *Nomina Sacra in the Greek Papyri of the First Five Centuries* (Leyden, 1959); this gives references to and discussions of work that appeared subsequent to Traube's book, and lists all instances up to the end of the fifth century.

Schuyler Brown, *Concerning the Origin of the Nomina Sacra* in *Studia Papyrologica* 9 (1970), pp. 7 ff.

There are useful lists supplementary to Paap by J. O'Callaghan, *Nomina Sacra in Papyris Graecis Neotestamentariis Saeculi III*, *Analecta Biblica* 46 (1970), (Rome, 1970) and by the same author for the fourth to the eighth centuries in *Studia Papyrologica* 10 (1971), pp. 99–122.

[2] Traube, op. cit., p. 6.

word in two letters would be occupied in drawing the line.⌉ Thus there is no connection with the abbreviations by suspension found in Greek documents[1] or with those found not in ordinary literary papyri but in working copies and a few technical texts.[2] The words in question are certain proper names and some other terms which for religious reasons only are given special treatment in writing. They divide into three classes; the first consists of the four words Ἰησοῦς, Χριστός, κύριος, θεός the abbreviation of which in their sacral meaning may be said to be invariable, the second of three words— πνεῦμα, ἄνθρωπος, σταυρός—of which the contracted form is found relatively early and relatively frequently, the third of the remainder. Of these eight words—πατήρ, υἱός, σωτήρ, μήτηρ, οὐρανός, Ἰσραήλ, Δανείδ, Ἰερουσαλήμ—the contraction is irregular; the problem here for the scribe was to determine when a word such as υἱός was used sacrally, e.g. in the expression Son of Man, or in an ordinary sense, or when a proper name such as David was used in a messianic context or in a purely historical one. The same problem arose to some extent with the four key words; in some Old Testament manuscripts, for example, Joshua is treated as a *nomen sacrum* since in Hebrew and Greek the name is identical with that of Jesus.

The different treatment accorded to these three groups may be seen in the great uncials and also in the Codex Purpureus Petropolitanus[3] where the four primary words together with πατήρ, πνεῦμα, and υἱός are in gold, the remaining five (out of the possible eight treated as *nomina sacra* in this manuscript) in silver. It is noteworthy, too, that only the first four are regularly contracted in early Latin manuscripts.[4]

Two other observations may be in place here. Firstly, the contractions[5] occur in documents as well as in literary manuscripts and where exceptions to the rule—rare even in documents[6]—are listed they will be found on examination to occur in private letters or prayers or in e.g. magical texts, often the work of an amateur or careless scribe. Secondly, there are a

[1] For these see now A. Blanchard, *Sigles et Abréviations dans les papyrus documentaires grecs* (*Bull. Inst. Clas. Stud., Suppl.* no. 30, 1974), who maintains that contraction is not a principle known to Greek systems of abbreviation.

[2] See E. G. Turner, *GMAW*, p. 17.

[3] Traube, op. cit., p. 22.

[4] See. C. H. Turner in *Miscellanea Ehrle* (*Studi e Testi*, 40, (1920)), iv, p. 64; 'Only the primary four . . . are everywhere and always abbreviated'.

[5] Suspensions as a rule are only found in the earliest period and soon disappear; for the very occasional suspension of θεός see H. C. Youtie's note on P. Mich. Inv. 337, 4 (late fourth century) in *ZPE* 22 (1976), p. 66.

[6] For eccentric forms in some documents see P. Merton ii. 93 and P. Abinn., p. 42.

few instances of words outside the standard list being contracted; some come from the pen of an obviously unskilled or ignorant scribe, but one or two (which will be examined later) occur in one of the earliest of all Christian papyri and witness to a stage at which the system was still to some extent fluid.

The *nomina sacra* have naturally been given close attention by palaeographers, but hopes that a detailed study of their variations might provide a clue to the provenance of manuscripts or their relationships have where the earliest period at any rate is concerned been disappointed.[1] But this in itself is negatively of interest; it suggests that, as we have reason to think on other grounds, the system did not grow up piecemeal but was originally laid down from a single centre. What is clear is that, as far as concerns the four primary words, the abbreviations occur, with such rare exceptions as to be insignificant, in written material of all kinds from the earliest period of which we have evidence, the first half of the second century; their universality is as striking as their antiquity.

The questions to which we want to find answers are as follows:

(1) Is the system Jewish or Christian in origin?
(2) If Christian, where and why did it originate and what is the earliest evidence for it?
(3) If these questions can be answered, what is the significance of the system for the history of the early Church in general and for that of the Church in Egypt in particular?

In one sense the answer to the first question is simple. The concept of the sacredness of the name of God and the related belief that this should in some fashion be expressed in the way the name was pronounced or written, though parallels can be found elsewhere, e.g. in magical texts of all kinds, is in this context indubitably Jewish; the ineffability of the name of God,

---

[1] Paap (op. cit., p. 126) has observed that οὐρανός, Δαυείδ, Ἰερυυσαλήμ, μήτηρ, σωτήρ are never found contracted in the Chester Beatty papyri, but as the last two are in any case late additions to the list too much importance should not be attached to this. H. Hunger has pointed out (*Anzeiger Akad. Wien* 13 (1960), p. 22) that the list of compendia in the Bodmer St. John (= H. 426) is practically identical with that in the Chester Beatty *Numbers* and *Deuteronomy*; this might suggest a common origin. He has also remarked that the treatment of *nomina sacra* in the Berlin Genesis (= H. 4) is very close to that in the two Chester Beatty manuscripts of Genesis (= H. 7 and 8). All three manuscripts are of much the same date; that in Berlin was purchased in Achmîm (Panopolis), the suggested provenance being the nearby White Monastery; two of the Bodmer papyri are demonstrably associated with Panopolis and if the Chester Beatty and the Bodmer papyri formed part of one and the same find, Panopolis would have been their *origo* (see E. G. Turner, *Greek Papyri*, pp. 52–3, and for an objection to this view see above, p. 7).

expressed when the Law was read in Hebrew by replacing the vowels proper to it by those of Adonai ('Lord'), is directly or indirectly the psychological origin of the *nomina sacra*; whether the Greek equivalents for the Hebrew words for God and Lord were ever written in contracted form by Jews is another question. Schuyler Brown has forcibly argued against Traube and others that there is no connection between the way in which the name is *written* in Hebrew and the writing of *nomina sacra* in Greek: there was nothing in the manner of writing it to distinguish it from other Hebrew words: the omission of vowels is neither here nor there since at this period this was common to all Hebrew writing, and in any case the *nomina sacra* do not omit all vowels and they do omit certain consonants: there was nothing ineffable about θεός and κύριος and the writing of them as *nomina sacra* would not affect the pronunciation.[1] Certainly there is no strict parallel between the method of writing the Name in Hebrew and the manner of writing the *nomina sacra* in Greek; but there are some indications, as we shall see, that not only the pronunciation but also the writing of the Name in Hebrew was regarded on occasion as requiring special attention.[2] And to assert that the form of writing e.g. κ̄c̄ would not affect the way it was spoken goes beyond what we know; all reading was reading aloud and the abbreviation would constitute a warning signal to the reader and may have served as the occasion for some mark of reverence on his part.

The question whether the Jews, when from the third century B.C. onwards they used a Greek translation of their scriptures wrote the contractions of θεός and κύριος, as in Traube's view they did, is a different one, and with the help of pre-Christian Jewish papyri from Egypt and that of the Biblical

[1] He considers that Christian scribes in writing *nomina sacra* were following a documentary practice whereby some proper names and titles were not always written in full; but in Greek documents of this period there are no contractions, only suspensions and above them there is no suprascript line, and the practice is quite unknown to literary manuscripts. A. Blanchard (op. cit., p. 18) also sees no connection between such *griffonnages* and *nomina sacra*; in fact, there is no real evidence in Greek documents for a habit of 'omitting the middle portion of an entire word'. Blanchard, however, follows Schuyler Brown in seeing no connection between the Hebrew tradition and *nomina sacra*. Byzantine documents do employ regular and systematic abbreviations, but, as Blanchard points out, the differences of form, date, and manner are too great for there to be any relationship here with the *nomina sacra*. See also below, p. 35, n. 2.

[2] It is important to distinguish between the writing and the speaking of the Name; while Origen (*in Ps.* 2: 2) tells us that the Name was read as Adonai (by the Hebrews) and as κύριος by the Greeks (i.e. Jews who knew no Hebrew), nothing is said or implied about the way it was written. All our evidence goes to show that in writing the Jews retained the Hebrew form.

texts, both Greek and Hebrew, discovered in the Dead Sea area of Palestine can now be given a decisively negative answer. From Egypt, from Qumran, and from another site in the wilderness of Judaea we now have seven manuscripts of the Jewish scriptures ranging from the early second century B.C. to the early first A.D. and all with one exception of the Law.[1] Not all preserve an instance of the Tetragrammaton, but two which do are substantial: the Cairo papyrus consisting of 115 fragments, three of Genesis and the rest of Deuteronomy, and the roll of the Twelve Minor Prophets from near Engedi with part of at least twenty-four columns. In none of these manuscripts is the Divine Name ever represented by κύριος; it is written in Hebrew. In some, as in that of the Minor Prophets, it is written in the Phoenician or ancient Hebrew characters, as it was still, according to Origen,[2] in the version of Aquila in the Roman period. The ancient Hebrew script had been largely abandoned after the exile; its retention is a mark of reverence for the Name and reflects the belief that this was the exact way in which it had been written by Moses.[3] In others, as in the Cairo Deuteronomy, it is written in the square Hebrew characters, which gave rise later to the mistaken transliteration of the four Hebrew letters as πιπι in Greek.[4] In one only, the roll of Leviticus from Qumran, do we find the Name itself written in Greek letters ΙΑΩ—hitherto known only from one later manuscript, the Codex Marchalianus of the Prophets. No line is drawn above the Name; the use of Hebrew in a Greek manuscript was warning enough. The other words that are treated as *nomina sacra* in later Greek manuscripts and are not of obviously Christian origin—*heaven, Israel, David, Jerusalem*—are without exception written in full.

With these texts may be associated a liturgical papyrus to be dated to the late first century A.D.;[5] it appears to be a

[1] The texts in question are as follows:
H. 38: Exodus, papyrus roll, Qumran, *c.* 100 B.C.
H. 46: Leviticus, papyrus roll, Qumran, late first century B.C.–early first century A.D.
H. 49: Leviticus, leather roll, Qumran, *c.* 100 B.C.
H. 51: Numbers, leather roll, Qumran, 50 B.C.–A.D. 50.
H. 56: Genesis/Deuteronomy, papyrus roll, P. Fouad Inv. 266, first century B.C.
H. 57: Deuteronomy, papyrus roll, P. Ryl. iii. 458, second century B.C.
H. 285: Dodekapropheton, parchment roll, desert of Judah, 50 B.C.–A.D. 50.
References to the publications with some later discussions will be found in van Haelst's *Catalogue.*
[2] In *Ps.* 2: 2. The ancient script is also used for the Name in the fragment of the Psalter dating from the third century A.D. in the version of Symmachus: see below, p. 32 n. 5.
[3] See W. H. Brownlee, *The Meaning of the Qumran Scrolls for the Bible* (New York, 1964), p. 29.   [4] See Traube, op. cit., pp. 28 ff.
[5] Published by P. Benoît in *Revue Biblique* 58 (1951), pp. 549 ff. (= H. 911): see Appendix I, p. 78.

prayer invoking the aid of the Angel of the Exodus against evil spirits. Both the subject-matter (to which parallels can be found in Philo) and the style of writing suggest a Jewish origin; and in it κύριος is written in full with no line above it, thus confirming Paap's view that the Jews had no occasion to regard κύριος as a *nomen sacrum*.[1] Only in the fourth century A.D. and later are there occasional examples of κύριος contracted in a Jewish manuscript; such cases are still exceptional and can be attributed to the influence of the usage prevailing in the world around them.

The treatment of the Tetragrammaton in the Hebrew manuscripts from Qumran is also relevant.[2] In the Isaiah scroll the Name is written in full; in a quotation from Isaiah in the Manual of Discipline four points are substituted for the Name,[3] while in the Habakkuk commentary the ancient Phoenician characters are employed for writing the Name only as they are in the Hymns scroll with one exception when the scribe forgot and put the square characters instead. And if we can trust Josephus,[4] in some manuscripts—no doubt reserved for ceremonial use—the name might be written in letters of gold.

From time to time the Name in Hebrew was abbreviated both in Hebrew manuscripts and when it was written in Hebrew in Greek manuscripts. A Greek papyrus from Oxyrhynchus of the third century A.D.[5] exhibits it in the form of a double *yod* with a line through it; other forms of abbreviation occur in the Elephantine Aramaic papyri of the fifth century B.C., in two late manuscripts, and on coins (though coins are not good witnesses to manuscript practice). It could be argued that there is a link between these occasional abbreviations of the Hebrew Tetragrammaton and the *nomina sacra*, but it is improbable. Not only are the abbreviations of the Hebrew Name very far

---

[1] At one time P. Kahle regarded the use of κύριος in a manuscript as a sure sign of Christian origin (see *Theol. Lit. Zt.* 1954, II, p. 2), but subsequently changed his mind and in *The Cairo Geniza*[2] (London, 1959), p. 219 claimed P. Oxy. iv. 656 for Judaism. What is true is that the contracted form of κύριος is in the first three centuries the mark of a Christian manuscript.

[2] See M. Delcor, *Des diverses manières d'écrire le tétragramme sacré dans les anciens documents hébraïques* in *Rev. Hist. Relig.* 147 (1955), pp. 149–73.

[3] For this see the comments of Françoise Dunand in *Papyrus grecs bibliques* (Cairo, 1966), p. 43; it is possible that the Name had to be inserted by someone other than the scribe of the manuscript.

[4] *Ant.* xii. 2. 10: cf. Clem. Alex. *Strom.* vi. 11. 84, and L. Blau *Studien zum althebräischen Buchwesen* (Strasburg, 1902), pp. 157 ff. A passage in the letter of Aristeas, § 176—ἡ νομοθεσία γεγραμμένη χρυσογραφίᾳ τοῖς Ἰουδαϊκοῖς γράμμασιν—has been taken to refer to the use of gold for the Tetragrammaton.

[5] P. Oxy. vii. 1007 (= H. 5): see Appendix 1, p. 77.

from being regular as are those of θεός and κύριος, but there is no one method of abbreviation and there is no suprascript line.[1] Thus the writing as well as the pronunciation of the Name might be accorded special treatment in Hebrew, but not invariably and not in a constant form. The form which this principally took was the use, as Origen correctly states,[2] of the archaic Hebrew characters; there is of course no parallel to this in Greek manuscripts, and we can conclude that there is no legacy from the Hebrew scribes to the writers of *nomina sacra*.

Graeco-Jewish manuscripts of the Roman and early Byzantine periods lead to the same conclusion. In some cases, as in that of the Oxyrhynchus papyrus just mentioned,[3] it is arguable whether the manuscript was Jewish or Christian in origin,[4] and it will be convenient to look first at those which are certainly Jewish. The earliest is a fragment now in Vienna of a parchment roll dated to the third or fourth century carrying some verses of the Psalms in the version of Symmachus;[5] here the Tetragrammaton appears in the ancient Hebrew characters and θεός and Ἰσραήλ are uncontracted. Other manuscripts which are incontestably Jewish are the fragments of Kings and Psalms in the version of Aquila from the Geniza of Cairo and assigned to the fifth or sixth century.[6] In both the Tetragrammaton appears in the ancient Hebrew characters, but in the Kings fragment there is a single instance of κύριος contracted to κ̅υ̅ at the end of a line and three of Ἰσραήλ contracted

---

[1] See Dunand, op. cit., pp. 39 ff. for an account of the different forms and letter shapes of the Name in Greek and Hebrew manuscripts from the Dead Sea area in relation to the Cairo papyrus. Delcor (op. cit., p. 157) draws attention to a passage in the Damascus document where the Tetragrammaton is referred to by the first two letters; but there is no contraction.

[2] *In Psalm.* 2: 2. In the early part of this often cited passage Origen is referring to the pronunciation, not to the writing, of the Name among Ἑβραῖοι (i.e. Jews whose language was Hebrew) and Ἕλληνες (i.e. Jews whose language was Greek). He then goes on to discuss the writing of the Name as follows: καὶ ἐν τοῖς ἀκριβεστάτοις δὲ τῶν ἀντιγράφων ἑβραϊκοῖς χαρακτῆρσιν κεῖται τὸ ὄνομα, ἑβραϊκοῖς δὲ οὐ τοῖς νῦν ἀλλὰ τοῖς ἀρχαιοτάτοις. It is clear from the context that he is talking of Greek manuscripts in use by Jews. It is usually thought that he had Aquila's version in mind, and this may well be so; but this form of the Tetragrammaton occurs in a fragment of Symmachus' version (see p. 30, n. 2 above) and Origen's statement could equally well apply to manuscripts of the LXX. In any case, he is here concerned not with versions, but with manuscripts.

Similarly when Jerome (*Ep. XXV ad Marcellam* and in his preface to Samuel (Migne, *PL* xxviii. 550) alludes to the use of the square Hebrew characters or to that of the *antiquae litterae* in both cases he is talking of Graeco-Jewish, not Christian manuscripts.

[3] p. 31, n. 1 above.

[4] See Appendix 1, pp. 74 ff.

[5] = H. 167. Both the format and the version, apart from the treatment of the *nomina sacra*, speak for its Jewish origin.

[6] = H. 74, 123, 203, 236.

to ισλ̄, again at the end of a line.[1] Elsewhere they are written in full, as are θεός, ἄνθρωπος, υἱός, and Ἰερουσαλήμ. In the Psalms θεός, οὐρανός, πατήρ, υἱός, Δαυείδ, and Ἰσραήλ are all uncontracted. The fact that the Tetragrammaton appears in Hebrew shows clearly that (as Origen implies) in writing as distinct from pronunciation κύριος = Adonai was not thought of as a substitute.[2] The single case of the Greek contracted form, an exception which proves the rule, is due less to Christian influence (for then it would have been regularly used) than to the exigencies of space; the scribe had left himself no space to write the Hebrew and so had recourse to the form prevailing in the non-Jewish world. Similarly, in only one out of the twenty-seven instances of the Tetragrammaton is the supra-script line employed. There could be no better witness to standard Jewish practice than these texts from a Jewish synagogue.

Prevailing Christian practice and perhaps the advisability of not openly flouting it will explain the presence of κc and ισλ with no suprascript line in a public inscription of a Samaritan synagogue in Thessalonica of the fourth century, where however θεός is uncontracted.[3] And if G. D. Kilpatrick is correct in thinking that a liturgical text on a roll from Oxyrhynchus is Jewish rather than Christian,[4] then the presence in it of θ̄ν̄ is to be explained on the same basis.

There remain for consideration two Biblical texts, both of Genesis, both from Oxyrhynchus, one part of a papyrus codex of the second century, the other part of a parchment codex of the third century;[5] both may well be Jewish, although a case can also be made out for their being Christian.[6] In the first,

---

[1] Ἰερουσαλήμ appears once as Ιουσαλμ, again at the end of a line where space was short. It should be noted that Ἰσραήλ is uncontracted in one of the Qumran manuscripts: see P. W. Skehan in *Vetus Testamentum* iv (1956), pp. 155 ff.

[2] κύριος was on occasion used as a title for the deity by Jews, e.g. by Philo and in the liturgical papyrus mentioned above, p. 30, n. 5; but what was legitimate enough in a treatise or a liturgical text would be deemed inappropriate for a roll of the Law. See also Dunand, op. cit., p. 52 and, for Philo, the review of Dunand's work by J. van Haelst in *Chronique d'Égypte* 44 (1969), pp. 148 ff.; observing that it is used as a divine name in Wisdom and in 2 and 3 Maccabees he concludes that either the Tetragrammaton or κύριος might be written and that in Jewish circles in Alexandria two texts may have circulated, one with the Tetragrammaton, the other with κύριος. However, we have no early Jewish manuscript of these books and it may be significant that they were excluded from the Jewish canon.

[3] = H. 53.

[4] See *Greek, Roman and Byzantine Studies* 5 (1964), p. 222, n. 14. Whoever the writer of the papyrus was, it looks as though he may not have been at home with the system; he writes β̄c̄ for βασιλεύς while Ἰσραήλ was apparently written in full.

[5] P. Oxy. iv. 656 (= H. 13) and vii. 1007 (= H. 5); for the date of the first, see H. I. Bell in *HTR* xxxvii (1944), p. 201.

[6] See Appendix I, pp. 74 ff.

in one place where in a Christian manuscript κ͞c would normally stand the space was left blank, as though in expectation of a second hand inserting the Hebrew Tetragrammaton; in the event a second hand wrote κύριος unabbreviated. There are no other contractions. In the second, as has been noted above, the Tetragrammaton is represented by a double *yod* with a line through it, a form of abbreviation already known from Jewish coins of the second century B.C.; θεός is contracted in the usual way. While it is established that in their Greek manuscripts of the Old Testament the Jews invariably wrote the Name in Hebrew, it does not follow that all Greek manuscripts with the Hebrew Tetragrammaton are necessarily Jewish. We know from other sources that a Jewish form of Christianity persisted in Oxyrhynchus,[1] and a possible explanation of these two eccentric texts would be that they were the work of Jewish-Christian scribes.

Thus in the light of discoveries made since he wrote Traube's statement that θ͞c and κ͞c were certainly of Jewish-Hellenistic origin[2] can be seen to be erroneous; there is no evidence in favour of it and much against. Perhaps the most conclusive evidence is that of the Greek inscriptions from Palestine covering the period from Qumran to Bar Kokhba;[3] there are 184 instances of κύριος in a sacral sense and 109 of θεός and in not one is either word contracted. For the formal origin of the *nomina sacra* we must look elsewhere.

Granted, then, that the system was Christian in origin and not Jewish, we need to ask why and where it was invented and what is the earliest evidence for it. Two alternative hypotheses may be advanced. The first assumes—something that is by no means certain—that κύριος was the first word to be so abbreviated. We have to envisage a newly formed Christian congregation—not necessarily in Egypt—who as Hellenized Jews had heard the Law so read in Greek that (as Origen tells us)[4] the Name, while written in Hebrew was never pronounced but represented in reading either by Adonai or possibly by the Greek equivalent of Adonai, κύριος. Expelled from the syna-

---

[1] See below, p. 57.

[2] Op. cit., p. 34. In the absence of other evidence Traube relied on the magical papyri of the late third or fourth century A.D. in which there is a strong Jewish element, and he infers that the occasional *nomina sacra* in these texts are of Jewish origin. But the magical papyri are thoroughly syncretistic and contain Christian elements as well.

[3] See M. Schwabe–B. Lifshitz, *Beth Shearim II, The Greek Inscriptions* (Jerusalem, 1967); κύριος in the sacral sense occurs in no. 184, θεός in no. 109.

[4] *In Psalmos*, 2:2: λέγεται μὲν (sc. the Tetragrammaton) τῇ Ἀδωναὶ προσηγορίᾳ, οὐχὶ τούτου γεγραμμένου ἐν τῷ τετραγραμμάτῳ, παρὰ δὲ ῞Ελλησι τῇ κύριος ἐκφωνεῖται.

gogue they would lose any slight contact they might have had with Hebrew and, although they would have had no difficulty in acquiring texts of the Greek version of the scriptures, when it came to copying them they would have no one competent to write the Name in Hebrew—in the synagogue a task probably reserved for the priest. The obvious course was to write κύριος; in imitation of the Hebrew the vowels of the stem of κύριος (together with one consonant) were omitted and a line placed above the contraction to warn the reader that the letters so marked could not be pronounced as they stood. It is at this point that the argument lacks conviction; would such a scribe have been aware of the absence of vowels in the Hebrew Name and, if he was anxious to follow Hebrew practice, why omit a consonant as well?[1] Leaving this objection on one side, we can see that on this theory κύριος in its religious significance would be clearly distinguished from its secular use, and in reading aloud this may have been recognised by some obeisance. The suprascript line was borrowed from Greek documentary practice. The use of abbreviation would then have been extended to other religious terms and names, a stage already reached in our earliest Christian papyri, for on this hypothesis the first step, that of contracting κύριος, would have been taken before the end of the first century.

There is, however, a more probably hypothesis. The earliest direct evidence for a compendium of a *nomen sacrum* comes not in a manuscript but in a literary source. In the Epistle of Barnabas the number of Abraham's followers recorded in two passages of Genesis as 318 is given a symbolic interpretation;[2] the Greek letter *tau* (of which the numerical value is 300) represents the cross, and the *iota eta* (the combined numerical value of which is 18) stand for Ἰησοῦς.[3] The writer does not put forward his

---

[1] The form κρ̄ς̄ occurs in only one Christian text and that not one of the earliest: see Paap, op. cit., p. 102. It is also found in P. Colon. Inv. 4780 (= H. 1072), the remarkable biography of Mani preserved in a miniature parchment codex of the fifth century. While the standard forms of *nomina sacra* for Ἰησοῦς, Χριστός, πνεῦμα, πατήρ, and ἄνθρωπος are regularly employed, κς̄ is used of Mani himself in 14. 4; this may explain why the form κρ̄ς̄ appears in 18. 11 when the reference is to the deity.

[2] The number symbolism is in itself sufficient to dispose of G. Rudberg's thesis (*Eranos* xiii (1913), pp. 156 ff.) that the system derives from documentary practice. Words may be slurred over in hastily written documents, but this led to no regular or systematic abbreviation; Christian manuscripts are not as a rule hastily or carelessly written and not infrequently a blank space surrounds the contracted *nomen sacrum* so that there is in effect no saving of space. Had saving either of time or space been the object, we should expect the system to be applied to the commonest words such as the definite article or the verb *to be*. To say with Rudberg that early Christian manuscripts are more akin to ostraca than to later manuscripts is very wide of the mark (Rudberg, quoted with approval by Paap, op. cit., p. 107 n. 12).

[3] *Tau* as a symbol for the cross is found both in other Christian and in pagan (e.g. Lucian, Δίκη Συμφώνων 12) writings, but is never treated in any manuscript as a *nomen sacrum* for

explanation of the number as a novelty and this might suggest that the abbreviation was current before it was given a symbolic interpretation. The epistle, which was regarded as canonical in some circles, is ascribed by modern scholars to dates ranging from A.D. 70 to 130, while a date about A.D. 100 is generally favoured; it is reasonable to conclude that $\overline{\iota\eta}$ as a compendium for 'Ιησοῦς goes back if not to the Apostolic at least to the sub-Apostolic age. It is generally assumed that the Epistle is of Alexandrian origin, but unfortunately there is no proof of this. Could it be proved, it would be valuable testimony to the existence of orthodox Christianity near the turn of the century, that is, in the dark period of the Alexandrian Church.[1]

It will be noticed that this compendium for 'Ιησοῦς is a suspension, not a contraction; that is, it is formed of the first two letters, not of the first and last, as indeed it had to be to give the required numerical value. Although the contracted form $\overline{\iota c}$ or $\overline{\iota\eta c}$ is far commoner and later became the only form used, the suspension $\overline{\iota\eta}$ is found in seven Christian papyri with forty-five instances in all.[2] One of them is the Egerton Gospel, the earliest Christian papyrus in which the name Jesus occurs (it does not come in the surviving fragment of the Rylands St. John) and another in the following century is the Chester Beatty Gospel and Acts.[3] Early as the usage is, it does not follow that there was a development from suspension to contraction; the manuscript evidence for $\overline{\iota c}$ or $\overline{\iota\eta c}$ is nearly as early as that for $\overline{\iota\eta}$. $\overline{\iota c}$ is found in the Chester Beatty Numbers and Deuteronomy and then in P. Oxy. iii. 405[4] and in the Bodmer St. John.[5] The form $\overline{\iota\eta c}$ (which as the oblique cases indicate, is a

σταυρός; $\overline{\tau} = $ σταυρός would have invited confusion with $\overline{\tau} = $ τριακόσιοι. (The closest approximation is $\overline{\sigma\rho\iota}$ with the *tau* and *rho* in ligature, found occasionally from the third century onwards, cf. Paap, op. cit., p. 112). Thaw (Tau) as the last letter of the Hebrew alphabet has been thought to have apocalyptic significance, as does omega in Greek, e.g. in Ezekiel 9: 4 where it is the mark on the forehead of the elect. For Christians, however, it was the symbol, not of the End, but of the cross (see F. Dornseiff, *Das Alphabet in Magie und Mysterium*[2] (Leipzig, 1925), p. 109). In a discussion of the significance of Thaw in Ezekiel and other passages E. Dinkler in *Zt. f. Theol. u. Kirche* 48 (1951), pp. 118–77, regards its use as an *Eigentums- und Schutzzeichen* as the origin of σρι; but given the general pattern of *nomina sacra* this is an unnecessary hypothesis. For a discussion of the different forms of abbreviating σταυρός and their frequency see K. Aland, *Studien zur Überlieferung des Neuen Testaments und seines Textes* (Berlin, 1967), pp. 173 ff.

[1] W. Bauer, for whose theory the Alexandrian origin of Barnabas would otherwise be an embarrassment, attempts unconvincingly to label it as Gnostic on the ground of its anti-Jewish attitude and allegorical interpretation of the Old Testament. It is hardly probable that an epistle recognised as Gnostic would have been accorded quasi-canonical status as it is e.g. in the Codex Sinaiticus where it is placed immediately after the Apocalypse; and a definition of Gnosticism as wide as Bauer's deprives the term of any definite meaning.   [2] See Paap, op. cit., p. 102.

[3] H. 371.   [4] H. 671.   [5] H. 426.

contraction, not a suspension) also occurs in the Chester Beatty Numbers and Deuteronomy and in the Chester Beatty Gospels and Acts side by side with $\overline{\iota\eta}$; it may have been an intermediate form between $\overline{\iota\eta}$ and $\overline{\iota c}$. On present evidence the form $\overline{\chi c}$ for $X\rho\iota\sigma\tau\acute{o}s$ is earlier than $\overline{\chi\rho}$ which is never found except in association with $\overline{\iota\eta}$ and then only in the Chester Beatty Gospels and Acts and in P. Oxy. viii. 1079.[1] There is thus no reason to think that with *nomina sacra* in general suspension is earlier than contraction. It seems then that there were two lines of development, the one owing something to number symbolism, the other, perhaps with an allusion to Alpha and Omega, taking the first and last letters. If, as looks probable enough, $'I\eta\sigma o\hat{u}s$ was the first name to be treated as a *nomen sacrum*,[2] the abbreviation $\overline{\kappa c}$ for $\kappa\acute{u}\rho\iota os$ would have been formed by analogy from it.[3]

More significant for our present purposes than this divergence of usage is the misuse of $\overline{\iota c}$ for $'I\eta\sigma o\hat{u}s$ in the Chester Beatty Numbers and Deuteronomy where it is regularly used, together with the form $\overline{\iota\eta c}$, of Joshua. Its use for Jesus was so well established in the second half of the second century that to write it wherever the name occurred was second nature to the scribe. This again would seem to carry the system back to at least the turn of the century; it is worth noting that at any rate it antedates the full development of Christian scholarship in Alexandria.

It was remarked earlier that the use of the compendium for the four primary words—$\theta\epsilon\acute{o}s$, $\kappa\acute{u}\rho\iota os$, $'I\eta\sigma o\hat{u}s$, $X\rho\iota\sigma\tau\acute{o}s$—was for all practical purposes invariable. A nice exception that proves the rule is provided by a papyrus from Oxyrhynchus; on the back of an account of corn dated to the first half of the third century, some one wrote a hymn to the Trinity, otherwise unknown, with musical notation;[4] here necessarily each syllable must be written out in full and in consequence $\theta\epsilon\acute{o}s$ is

---

[1] H. 559. The form $\overline{\chi}$ recorded in a Strasburg liturgical text (= H. 998) of the fourth or fifth century (Paap, op. cit., p. 109) is replaced in C. del Grande's edition (*Liturgiae Preces Hymni Christianorum* (Naples, 1934), p. 6) by $\overline{\chi\upsilon}$: see Appendix V.

[2] Both the precedence of $'I\eta\sigma o\hat{u}s$ over other *nomina sacra* and of the suspended form over the contracted may be implicit in a passage of Clement of Alexandria. He writes (*Strom.* 6. 278 ff.): φασὶν οὖν εἶναι τοῦ μὲν κυριακοῦ σημείου τύπον κατὰ τὸ σχῆμα τὸ τριακοσιοστὸν στοιχεῖον, τὸ δὲ ἰῶτα καὶ τὸ ἦτα τοὔνομα σημαίνειν τὸ σωτήριον. The φασὶν εἶναι suggests that $\overline{\iota\eta}$ was no longer current in Clement's day. The editors of P. Lond. Christ. (p. 3) quote G. B. de Rossi (*Bull. di Arch. Crist.*, S. iv, vi. 37) to the effect that $\overline{\iota\eta}$ was in use from the Apostolic age onwards.

[3] κύριος is very occasionally suspended, but never in the second century; it is found in a few occasional texts (prayers and letters) and in the Berlin Genesis (= H. 4) where in six instances it was corrected; it also occurs once by what is clearly a scribal error in the Chester Beatty Gospels and Acts (see Paap, op. cit., p. 102).

[4] P. Oxy. xv. 1786 = H. 962.

uncontracted.¹ The general principle can be best illustrated by the treatment of 'Ιησοῦς when the reference is to Jesus. In 1959 Paap had noted¹ that, down to the end of the fifth century, in its sacral meaning it was found abbreviated 976 times in 76 sources as against 10 places in 9 sources where it was written in full. On inspection the exceptions are more apparent than real; three are prayers (private texts), three are magical and two amulets (not necessarily of Christian origin), one is a medical miscellany written for private use, while the last exception rests on an uncertain reading.² Thus there is no certain instance of the name in its sacral sense being left uncontracted in any text of the New Testament or indeed in any book as distinct from occasional and private papers.³

One might reasonably expect that the earliest group of Christian papyri—those listed above on pp. 13–14 as assignable to the second century—would throw some light on the origin and development of the system. At first glance the results are disappointing; with two exceptions, no. 4 of which more than fifty leaves or parts of leaves survive and no. 11 with sixty lines, the earliest papyri are very fragmentary and in no less than five out of fourteen there is no occurrence of a *nomen sacrum*. θεός, κύριος, 'Ιησοῦς, Χριστός are regularly contracted;⁴ πνεῦμα is found once and correctly contracted in no. 8 and incorrectly in no. 4. The contraction of πατήρ in the sacral sense goes back to the second century, witness nos. 11 and 13; it has perhaps some claim to be regarded as one of the original group. Later on usage becomes irregular and often inconsistent, especially in sub-literary or non-literary texts such as prayers and letters, but this is hardly surprising with a word so often employed in a purely secular sense. Evidence for the early contraction of ἄνθρωπος can be found in no. 4; on the

---

¹ Op. cit., p. 107.

² In P. Oxy. ix. 1170 (= H. 357), a papyrus codex of Matthew of the late fourth or fifth century A. S. Hunt read in ll. 32–3 [οτε ετελεσεν ο Ιη|σους δι]ατ[ασ]σων. But to read [οτε ετελεσεν ο | ιης δι]ατ[ασ]σων would suit the spacing better; similarly in l. 42 ιης ει]πεν would fit as well as ιησουσ ει]πεν, particularly when it is remembered that a small space was often left before and after a contraction. In l. 38 [ω τα ερ]γα του χρι[σ]το[υ the papyrus (now Bodl. MS. Gr. bibl. d. 6 (P)), is all but illegible, but to assume a reading χρυ would result in too short a line.

³ In his list of *nomina sacra* in third-century texts of the New Testament O'Callaghan (see p. 26 n. 1) cites one instance of 'Ιησοῦς written out from the Bodmer codex of Luke and John (= H. 406) at John 6: 11. The *ed. pr.* here reads ο ι]η[σ]ου[ς και ευχαριστησα]ς [δι]εδω on which the editors commented *lectio valde dubia; alibi undique compendio utitur librarius*. The photograph suggests that the correct reading here may be ο ι[ης κ]αι ευχαριστησας] δ[ι]εδω; the tip of the kappa in this hand is very like that of upsilon, and the abrasion of the surface would remove any traces of the superscript line above.

⁴ In n. 12, the Michigan fragment of *The Shepherd*, we find θεον [*sic*]; this is probably a scribal error since considerations of space make it certain that κύριος was contracted.

other hand, the earliest instance of the contraction of υἱός is in the Chester Beatty Pauline Epistles[1] and the Bodmer St. John,[2] the only second-century text in which the word occurs in a sacral sense being no. 8 where it is uncontracted. That conveniently careless penman, the scribe of no. 4, quite incorrectly contracts Ἰσραήλ; hence we can again infer that the correct use of this compendium is older than the papyrus, and it is likely that what goes for Ἰσραήλ would also go for Δαυείδ. Here there may be an important clue to the origin of the system.

More evidence on this point comes from no. 11, the Egerton Gospel in the British Library. Side by side with the familiar compendia are three that are unique: $\overline{M\omega} = M\omega\ddot{\upsilon}\sigma\hat{\eta}s$, $\overline{H[\Sigma A\Sigma}$ = Ἠσαίας, $\overline{\Pi PO\Phi A\Sigma}$ = προφήτας,[3] and one not unique but very rare, $\overline{BA\Lambda EY[\Sigma I}$ = βασιλεῦσι.[4] In any period there are very occasional eccentric forms, most of which occur once only and then usually in a badly written manuscript, the result of the misunderstanding or vagaries of a particular scribe;[5] but both the early date and the connectedness of this group set them apart. It seems to represent an experimental phase in the history of the system when its limits were not clearly established, though the basic words were; $\overline{M\omega}$ is clearly formed on the analogy of $\overline{IH}$. By the end of the second century the list had been pruned and effectively closed.

One word that appears to be a late addition to the list and whose absence from the earliest texts may be significant is σωτήρ.[6] As a title of Jesus in the New Testament it is confined to

---

[1] = H. 497.   [2] = H. 426.

[3] ἐπρόφοεν (l. 55) clearly derives from the compendium for προφήτης just as $\overline{\sigma\rho\theta\eta}$ in the Bodmer St. John does from $\overline{\alpha\rho\sigma}$.

[4] For two other instances, one in a Greek, the other in a Coptic manuscript, the one of the fourth century, the other of the seventh or eighth, see Paap, op. cit., p. 114. The former has been claimed as a Jewish text (see above, p. 33 n. 4), but the Christian associations of the contraction tell against the hypothesis. This occasional treatment of βασιλεύς as a *nomen sacrum* may have been inspired by Rev. 19: 16 where the Word of God has written on his robe and on his thigh the title βασιλεὺς βασιλέων καὶ κύριος κυρίων.

[5] Subsequently to those noted by Paap, op. cit., pp. 114–15 the publication of P. Bodmer vii and viii has yielded Μιχαηλ, νωε, σαρρα and αβρααμ while P. Bodmer xiii has added αδαμ, δυιν, δυω, δυι and αβρμ. The last group apart, these are not abbreviations and the supra-script line may indicate not so much a *nomen sacrum* as the presence of a non-Greek word. The scribe of P. Bodmer vii and viii was both amateurish (as his hand makes evident) and ignorant, and not much importance should be attached to his practice. This group of Bodmer manuscripts—v, vii, viii, xi, and xiii—in which at least two scribes were involved have an exceptional number of unusual forms of the regular *nomina sacra*. $\overline{\alpha\gamma\iota\omega}$ $\overline{\pi\nu\iota}$ in P. Bodmer xii (which, unlike the editor, I should not attribute to the scribe of vii, viii, and xi) may well be accidental (but see Paap, op. cit., p. 124). Of more interest (see below, p. 40 n. 3) is the form ιχθυς in the Coptic codex iii. 2 from Nag Hammadi (ed. A. Böhlig and F. Wisse (Leiden, 1975), p. 166) to which I know of no parallel; here the line must denote a *nomen sacrum*.

[6] O'Callaghan (op. cit., p. 79) in his analysis of the compendia found in third-century texts of the New Testament observes that no compendium of this word occurs; but it is relevant that all the instances bar one are secular.

the Pauline and Lukan writings apart from one passage in the
Fourth Gospel and several in the late second epistle of Peter; its
strong pagan associations would have made it distasteful to
Jewish Christians and later the use of it by Gnostic sects to
designate the divine liberator from the evil powers of this
world may have restricted its employment in other circles.

The question of why some theological terms, the inevitable
four apart, were selected for this treatment and others ignored
has attracted little attention.[1] The list is limited to proper
names and nouns, in two cases with their associated adjectives
and in one with a verb;[2] but even so there are some surprising
omissions. Why should λόγος or even σοφία be excluded? More
striking still is the omission of the eucharistic words αἷμα,
ἄρτος, οἶνος, σάρξ, σῶμα, an omission that was sometimes
felt as can be seen from the Chester Beatty Pauline Epistles
of the early third century in which at Hebrews 9: 13 a line
is placed above αἷμα, though the word itself is not contracted.[3]
The omission of these words and of λόγος points to a very
early date for the list and to an area where Pauline and
Johannine influence had not penetrated. Yet another pointer in
the same direction may be the presence of ἄνθρωπος in the list
at an early date. It is found in the Chester Beatty Numbers and
Deuteronomy, once again in a secular sense which implies that
its use as a sacral term is earlier. Gnostic usage apart, it must
owe its position to the title of Jesus as Son of Man, employed
by the evangelists only in reporting sayings of Jesus. It has
been suggested that in the original Aramaic it may have
carried no particular significance; it seems likely that the
nomen sacrum, whether or no based on a misunderstanding, goes
back to the translations into Greek of Aramaic Gospels or
sayings. For our present purpose what is significant is that
the title is of Jewish origin, is never found in St. Paul, and
disappears as a title relatively soon.

---

[1] The question is raised but no answer advanced by O'Callaghan (op. cit., p. 27, n. 28),
who asks why only fifteen were selected and why these fifteen; he draws attention to the illogi-
cality of not treating βασιλεύς as a *nomen sacrum* in an expression such as ὁ βασιλεὺς τοῦ Ἰσραήλ
where Ἰσραήλ is a *nomen sacrum* only by virtue of βασιλεύς (see above, p. 33, n. 4). In this context
it is worth noting that both βασιλεύς and Μωϋσῆς (whose omission from the list is singled out
by O'Callaghan) are found contracted in the Egerton Gospel.

[2] χριστός → χριστιανός,   πνεῦμα → πνευματικός,   σταυρός → σταυρόω   (and   compounds),
προφήτης → προφητεύω (both in the Egerton Gospel only).

[3] For a few other instances including ἰχθύς (fourth century) and σάρξ (seventh century)
see Paap, op. cit., p. 114.

[4] Cf. G. Vermes' appendix to M. Black, *An Aramaic Approach to the Gospels and Acts*[3] (Oxford,
1967), pp. 310–30, cited and discussed by C. H. Dodd, *The Founder of Christianity* (London,
1971), pp. 110–13.

Behind the list, at any rate as composed of the four primary words with πνεῦμο, πατήρ, ἄνθρωπος, Ἰσραήλ and probably Δαυείδ, σταυρός, υἱός lies a quite unmistakeable, if implicit, theology. The character of this theology, its source, and the authority on which it rests call for a brief scrutiny. The problem of authority has been succinctly stated by T. C. Skeat:[1] 'The significant fact', he writes, 'is that the introduction of the *nomina sacra* seems to parallel very closely the adoption of the papyrus codex; and it is remarkable that this development should have taken place at about the same time as the great outburst of critical activity among Jewish scholars which led to the standardization of the text of the Hebrew Bible. It is no less remarkable that this seems to indicate a degree of organization, of conscious planning, and uniformity of practice among the Christian communities which we have hitherto had little reason to suspect and which throws a new light on the early history of the Church.' It is worth bearing in mind Ulrich Wilcken's comment, made more than sixty years ago, that the *nomina sacra* were the spontaneous invention of an individual who was looking for an outward form to separate the holy words in Biblical manuscripts from the rest of the text and for this reason made a deliberate and conscious attempt to avoid ordinary methods of writing.[2] Wilcken's view has sometimes been dismissed as an explanation that explains nothing, but it is rash to dismiss the considered judgment of a scholar whose wide historical perspective was matched with such detailed knowledge of the documents of the Hellenistic world.

The profound religious significance of the Name as denoting equally the person and the power of him who bears it is evident enough in the New Testament.[3] We may think, for example, not only of the famous passage in Philippians 2: 9—'that at the name of Jesus every knee shall bow'—but more particularly of the stress laid on the Name in Luke's account of the primitive community in Jerusalem.[4] In the present context some passages in the Apocalypse are directly relevant, e.g. 7: 1–4 where the servants of God are sealed with the Name on their foreheads, and 14: 1 where the names are those of the Lamb and his Father;

[1] In 'Early Christian Book Production' in the *Cambridge History of the Bible*, ii, pp. 72–3.
[2] L. Mitteis–U. Wilcken, *Grundzüge und Chrestomathie der Papyrusurkunden* (Leipzig, 1912), i, pp. xliv–v. T. C. Skeat (op. cit., p. 72) is inclined to attribute the invention of the papyrus codex as a vehicle for Christian manuscripts as well as that of the *nomina sacra* to some 'dominating genius at work in the field of the earliest Christian literature'.
[3] In addition to the passages cited below cf., e.g., John 17: 12 and for the identity of name and person I Clement 59, 3.
[4] Acts, 1–7.

again in 19: 1–6 the Word of God has written on him 'a name known to none but himself' and on his robe and thigh were written King of Kings and Lord of Lords. Such sealings or χαρακτῆρες were composed, as were often names on coins, of the initial two or three letters,[1] and these passages about 'sealing with the Name' may well presuppose the existence of ιη̄ or ιη̄ς. Indeed the Apocalypse may have been written after the system was established.

In the next two generations the significance of the Name was yet further emphasized. Speculations on Christ as the Name, i.e. the Tetragrammaton, were current in Christian Jewish circles in Egypt if, as seems likely, the apocryphal letter of James is of Egyptian provenance.[2] In Rome Hermas (whose book, *The Shepherd*, was much read in Egypt) wrote: 'the Tower (i.e. the Church) has been founded by the utterance of the almighty and glorious Name'.[3] This particular emphasis is characteristic of, though not confined to, Jewish-Christian theology; thus Cardinal Daniélou, observing that 'the Name . . . was for the primitive Christian community a designation of Christ as Word of God incarnate' goes on to point out that the Gospel of Truth (a second-century homily that may be an early work of the Egyptian Gnostic Valentinus) is yet more explicit, 'now the Name of the Father is the Son'.[4]

Where are theological conceptions such as these first likely to have been given symbolic form in manuscripts? Alexandria has been suggested as a focal point of Jewish mysticism and as a centre, if not *the* centre of the Graeco-Roman book trade, perhaps too because our earliest surviving Christian manuscripts come from Egypt, though this is but the accident of survival. None the less, I think the case for Alexandria can be dismissed. Early Christian writers had little to do with the international book trade; more to the point, it is hard to credit that a church as relatively obscure as that of Alexandria seems to have been in the first century or so of its existence, with no great name recorded in the annals of the sub-Apostolic age, could have exercised so powerful and lasting an influence throughout the

---

[1] For the abbreviation of the Tetragrammaton on Jewish coins see M. Delcor, loc. cit.

[2] See G. Quispel, *Gnostic Studies* (Istanbul, 1974/5), II, p. 229, referring to L. Cerfaux in *Recueil L. Cerfaux* (Paris, 1954), vol. ii, pp. 125–58.

[3] *Sim.* ix. 14. 3: *Vis.* iii. 3. 1. These passages are cited by R. M. Grant in *Gnosticism and Early Christianity* (New York, 1959), p. 67. He further points out that in Hermas' theology the Son of God is identified with the Holy Spirit, the Name of God, and the Law of God; he sees in these passages the influence of early Jewish mysticism leading through Valentinian speculations in due course to Gnostic heresies (cf. also Quispel, op. cit., i, p. 208).

[4] *Primitive Christian Symbols* (English translation (London, 1964)), p. 142.

Greek Christian world.¹ A further argument against an Alexandrian origin is that in Coptic manuscripts only the four basic words, together occasionally with πατήρ and πνεῦμα are abbreviated, more or less as in Latin. Had the system been of Alexandrian origin we would have expected the Coptic church to have followed the Greek practice, but it did not. Again, while I believe it a mistake to hold, as many scholars do, that down to the middle of the second century or beyond the Egyptian Church was essentially Gnostic (and hence the silence in our authorities), yet Gnosticism was undoubtedly very influential; why then are there no specifically Gnostic *nomina sacra* (we might think of Buthos, Pleroma, or Phaos) and why are the Old Testament terms such as Israel and David included? When we first meet with actual Gnostic texts, their writers accept the established *nomina sacra* and do not add to them; this is intelligible if they originated outside Egypt and go back to the first century.

Rome as the source of the *nomina sacra* is even less plausible than Alexandria. It is not just that the compendium for *Christus* appears in Latin manuscripts in its Greek, not a Latin dress—this might be put down, if unconvincingly, to the influence of Greek on the liturgy of the Roman church; it is much more that our earliest Latin Christian manuscripts either do not employ *nomina sacra* or do so in an uncertain or irregular fashion. Later the contraction of the four primary words became well established; but in the oldest of these manuscripts, a leaf from a liturgical codex,² *pater* and *dominus* are twice written in full. In others, for example in a Latin version of Exodus from Egypt,³ contracted and uncontracted forms of *deus* and *dominus* are found side by side, while in the Psalmus Responsorius in Barcelona⁴ we find the forms *iesum* and *dei* together with five other *nomina sacra* written out with no suprascript line; and whereas πατήρ and σταυρός are among the early Greek *nomina sacra* the contraction of *pater* and *crux* is unknown to Latin manuscripts. Equally, as C. H. Turner has noted,⁵ in all the older Gospel manuscripts even Israel, David, and Jerusalem

---

¹ A possible exception would be Barnabas (see above, p. 36); the evidence for St. Mark's association with Alexandria is too late to be relevant here (above, p. 59).

² P. Ryl. iii. 472 = H. 1211.   ³ P.S.I. xii. 1272 = H. 1203.

⁴ = H. 1210: cf. also P.S.I. xiii, 1300 (= H. 1208), a Graeco-Latin text of Ephesians (= H. 523) and P. Oxy. xviii. 2193 and 2194; for the practice of the Codex Bezae see E. A. Lowe, *Palaeographical Papers* (Oxford, 1972) i, pp. 226–7.

⁵ 'The *Nomina Sacra* in Early Latin MSS' in *Miscellanea Ehrle* iv (= *Studi e Testi*, 40 (Rome, 1924), p. 64. Writing before the discovery of the Latin fragments from Egypt mentioned above, Turner remarks that the only *nomina sacra* 'which in Latin are everywhere and always abbreviated are the four primary words (*deus, dominus, Iesus, Christus*). And nowhere and never

are invariably written in full, whether in the Old Latin or the Vulgate version. There can be no doubt that the system was originally alien to western Christendom and was not fully accepted, and then only with limitations, until the fifth century. Rome does not provide the answer for which we are looking.

The long historical contacts between Palestine and Egypt and the close religious associations between Alexandria and Jerusalem need no emphasis; but in themselves they are not sufficient to make it plausible that the system of *nomina sacra* originated in Jerusalem and thence spread to Egypt and everywhere where Greek was written.[1] There are more compelling reasons which point in this direction. Recent studies of the primitive Christian Church in Jerusalem, for which our principal source is Acts 2: 41–5: 42, and which grew out of the Jewish Hellenistic community, have drawn attention to the emphasis it laid on the Name of Jesus. L. Cerfaux has detected[2] what he describes as a rudimentary theology of the Name which has left its traces in early Christian literature; the position of the Apostles was that of dispensers of the power of the Name, the name of God and that of Jesus being realities equivalent and convertible.[3] This, in his view, determined the Christian interpretation of the Old Testament, every verse in the messianic passages where the Name occurred being carefully noted. Similarly J. Daniélou has emphasized the importance of the Name in Jewish-Christian theology; the Name was identified with the Messiah and so with Jesus.[4] It is a reasonable assumption that once the Gospel was put into writing in any form

in the early documents with which we are dealing are abbreviations found for *pater* or *mater*, to say nothing of *caelum* or *homo*, *crux* or *salvator*. Even *Israel*, *David*, and *Hierusalem* are always written in full in all our older Gospel MSS, whether of the Old Latin or the Vulgate'. Latin practice incidentally provides clear support for the division of the *nomina sacra* into two classes, primary and secondary.

[1] Antioch, where the name Christian was first used (Acts, 11: 26) might call for consideration were there any grounds for associating it with Alexandria and Egyptian Jewry.

[2] 'La première Communauté chrétienne' in *Recueil L. Cerfaux*, ser. 4, vol. ii, pp. 125 ff.; he suggests (p. 155) that Luke's account in these chapters derives from a separate written source. The theology of the Name is not, of course, peculiar to the primitive Jerusalem church, as Phil. 2: 9 and other Pauline passages demonstrate, but its beginnings may have been there.

[3] See above pp. 41–2.

[4] In his *History of Early Christian Doctrine I: Theology of Jewish Christianity* (English translation, J. A. Baker, London, 1964), esp. pp. 147 ff. In Daniélou's view the designation of Christ as the Name was 'one of the essential aspects of Jewish Christianity'; he sees this Jewish Christianity as Essene in character and as such opposed to Jewish orthodoxy with which James, an observant of the Law, was in sympathy; and to Essene Christians, in part at least, should be attributed the foundation of the Church of Alexandria some time after A.D. 70.

Not all the strands of evidence for these views are equally strong: e.g., unless we accept the wildly improbable view that the Qumran scrolls are Christian in origin there is nothing to support the statement that χ was used as a symbol of Χριστός in early times. For our present

some written emphasis on the Name followed naturally; and the treatment of the *nomina sacra* in the early papyri of the Old Testament corresponds to the attitude taken to it, according to these scholars, in the early communities.

We have already noted that Egyptian Christianity had a strong Jewish strain in it, a strain that persisted as the popularity of Hermas and of the Gospel of Thomas indicates.[1] In any case Jerusalem would have been the natural *fons et origo* of Egyptian Christianity, and it is not surprising that the *nomina sacra* found in our earliest papyri have a strongly Jewish flavour.[2] Israel and David established themselves early in what became the second category; more significant, perhaps, is the occurrence in the Egerton Gospel of Moses and Isaiah as *nomina sacra.* In the Qumran texts the Messiah is regarded as being a second Moses; what has been called the Moses typology is characteristic of Jewish Christianity which looks to Moses as the exemplar just as the universalist theology of St. Paul looks to Abraham. It may not be an accident that Pauline texts are not found in the earliest group with the single exception—if it is an exception—of the epistle to Titus.

W. D. Davies has suggested[3] that the faith was carried to Alexandria by Jewish Christians from Palestine, that is by the Christian community under the leadership of James (which he distinguishes both from the Ebionite ascetics and from Jewish Christians in general), and argues that to them the synagogue tradition was of great importance. As we have already remarked, the system of *nomina sacra* presupposes a degree of control and organization; the Jewish tradition of the synagogue *lector*,

purposes it makes little difference whether it was Essene Christians or followers of James who brought Christianity to Egypt: but I find it hard to credit that no move was made until after A.D. 70 and that the kind of authority required to lay down the guidelines for Christian scribes could have issued from anywhere except the circle of the apostles or their immediate successors.

Daniélou's view (op. cit., p. 52) that the Church in Alexandria was submerged in the Jewish colony and consequently shared in its sufferings has much in its favour (see below, pp. 45 ff.).

See also R. N. Longenecker, *The Christology of Early Jewish Christianity* (London, 1970), p. 17 for the identification of the Name with Jesus.

[1] As late as the fourth century we hear of a Christian of Oxyrhynchus going to church on the Sabbath (P. Oxy. vi. 903), a practice later visited with punishment (see H. Chadwick, *Priscillian of Avila* (Oxford, 1976), p. 75, n. 4).

[2] The use of the suprascript line above certain Old Testament names in P. Bodmer vii and viii (see above, p. 39, n. 5) might be thought to point to Jewish influence were it not that the scribe is so palpably amateurish; thus, while he normally contracts κύριος on one occasion he writes κυριω θεω (*sic*).

[3] In *Paul and Jewish Christianity* in *Judéo-christianisme . . . Hommages . . . J. Daniélou* (Paris, 1972), pp. 69 ff. If the reading of Codex Bezae at Acts 18: 25 which adds ἐν τῇ πατρίδι to κατηχημένος is accepted, Apollos was instructed in Alexandria before his meeting with Paul (cf. B. M. Metzger, *The Early Versions of the New Testament* (Oxford, 1977), p. 99).

the great care taken in writing and preserving the rolls of the Law, the institution of the Geniza, if carried over in a modified form to Jewish Christianity, would explain much about our earliest Christian manuscripts from Egypt.

Seen in this perspective the *nomina sacra* may be plausibly viewed as the creation of the primitive Christian community, representing what might be regarded as the embryonic creed of the first Church; the four primary terms (as they later became) together with πατήρ, σταυρός, and πνεῦμα represent the beliefs common to all Christians, some of the others the particular Jewish strain in the Jerusalem church.

That the *nomina sacra* are found in our earliest papyri suggests that the form of belief they enshrine, contrasting in some respects with Pauline Christianity, persisted in Alexandria well after A.D. 70. They would thus belong to the oldest stratum of the Christian faith and may well be contemporary with the first authorized or authoritative Christian writing. The establishment of the practice would not have been left to the whims of a single community, still less to that of an individual scribe. Everything would fall into place were we to assume that the guidelines for the treatment of the sacred names had been laid down by the Church at Jerusalem, probably before A.D. 70; they would carry the authority of the leaders of the Church as the first Gospels must have done. The system was too complex for the ordinary scribe to operate without either rules or an authoritative exemplar; otherwise the difficulty of determining which was a secular, which a sacred usage would have been considerable even in a small community.

Two other questions remain to which only the most tentative answers can be given. Was Ἰησοῦς as a *nomen sacrum* prior to κύριος or θεός and, if so, what was the form of the compendium? That the form ιη is so early suggests that it did not derive from κϲ as ιϲ might have done; they could have developed independently, but the authority behind them must have been the same and the argument from theology would support the priority of Ἰησοῦς. I suspect that the original form was ιηϲ or ιϲ and that ιη was devised to suit the number symbolism by which the particular passage in Genesis and possibly others too were interpreted.[1]

---

[1] For the application of number symbolism to Ἰησοῦς see F. Dornseiff, op. cit. (cf. p. 36), pp. 130–31; the numerical value of the Name was 888, the separate letters standing for 8, 10, 200, 70, 400, 200. From a different standpoint it was regarded as a perfect name, 888 being composed of eight units, eight tens, and eight hundreds.

F. Doelger has pointed out (*ΙΧΘΥΣ* I² (Munich, 1928), p. 356) that the passage in Barnabas

The second question is the more important and the more difficult. Are we to regard the all but universal adoption of the papyrus codex as the vehicle for the sacred books of Christianity and the invention and imposition of the system of *nomina sacra* as two quite separate developments, one hailing from Rome,[1] the other from Jerusalem? A good case can be made out for associating the use of the codex with Rome (and of Roman influence on the Church of Alexandria at a later date there can be no doubt); but a single source for the two would certainly be an economic hypothesis, and the alternative is that the papyrus codex originated in the tablets on which the oral law in Judaism, as distinct from the Torah, was recorded.[2] It is, however, a long step from the writing tablet to the papyrus codex as we know it at the beginning of the second century. *Non liquet.*

In form the *nomina sacra* cannot be explained as imitative of or even adapted from either Greek or Jewish scribal practice; they no more resemble the abbreviations or symbols in Greek documents or literary texts than they do the Jewish treatment of the Tetragrammaton. Like so much in early Christianity, they are *sui generis.* In intention they are strictly religious; the reverence for the Name derives from the Jewish background, as does much else in primitive Christianity. The combination of old and new is characteristic; we might instance the adoption of the Old Testament as basic Christian texts together with their translation into the form, that of the codex, already established for the new writings of the new religion. The attitude of mind that they express, somewhere on the borderline between religion and magic, while essentially Jewish, also looks forward to later developments in Catholic Christianity. They are a unique device that in the minimum of space provides a summary outline of theology. It has been suggested that they constitute a cryptographic system,[3] but for this they are too simple and too open and where cryptography was the object, Christians could do better than this, as the *sator—opera—rotas—tenet* formula is echoed both by Clement of Alexandria and by Hippolytus. He would attribute the abbreviation of the names Ἰησοῦς and Χριστός to the fact that they are both very common words (hardly an adequate explanation) and would derive the usage from Gnostic speculations on the names; in the middle of the second century the Marcosians (followers of Marcus, a disciple of Valentinus) equated Ἰησοῦς with iota, this being a perfect letter composed of $1+2+3+4$, though no suprascript line was attached. (For the Marcosians see Irenaeus, *Adversus Haereses* (ed. Harvey) 18, 12, p. 192.)

[1] See T. C. Skeat in *The Cambridge History of the Bible*, ii, pp. 73 ff., and the present writer in id. i, pp. 58–9.

[2] See the present writer in *The Codex* (*Proc. Brit. Acad.* 40 (1956), pp. 178, 188.

[3] So A. Blanchard, op. cit., p. 18. But would θ̄ς for θεός or ιη̄ς for Ἰησοῦς deceive anyone?

witnesses. At the same time their full meaning was only apparent to the faithful to whose attention it was brought whenever the sacred books, whether of the Old Testament or of those that later became the New, were read.

If this argument is sound, their significance for the history of the early Church is greater than has hitherto been appreciated. Cardinal Daniélou has observed[1] that the study of Jewish-Christian symbols supported by archaeological discoveries has made possible the writing of a new page in the history of Christianity in that obscure period that lies between the beginnings recorded in the Pauline Epistles and the Acts of the Apostles and the Church as we find it in the second century. To that page the *nomina sacra* contribute a footnote of some theological importance and at the same time shed some illumination, however sparse, on the dark period of the Church in Egypt.

[1] *Les Symboles chrétiens primitifs* (Eng. trans., D. Attwath (London, 1964), p. viii).

III

THE CHARACTER AND DEVELOPMENT
OF THE CHURCH

In the preceding chapter we have found reason to think that Christianity reached Egypt from Palestine in a form strongly influenced by Judaism. If this is correct, it may not in itself appear to answer either of the two questions to which we want to find answers: first, why is so little heard and known about the Church in Egypt in the first century and a half of its existence, and secondly, is it a plausible explanation of this state of affairs that the Church in its beginnings was entirely under Gnostic influence, an influence that later generations were anxious to disclaim? As for the second question, while the Jewish element in Gnosticism is thought to have been strong, the choice of words for treatment as *nomina sacra* hardly suggests that Jewish influence on the Church in Egypt was of that character; but as for the first, it might well be thought that a church founded from and in close touch with Jerusalem and active in a city that has been called 'the only spiritually productive centre of Israel'[1] would have made a mark in Christian history that would not have escaped later ages. In fact, it made no such mark.

The answer to the second question that has found most support in recent years is that first advanced by Walter Bauer in 1934.[2] The essence of the argument is that early Egyptian Christianity was Gnostic through and through: that, while there may have been individual Christians who were not Gnostics, orthodox Christianity did not find a firm footing in Egypt till well on in the second century: that in consequence the early history of the church was later hushed up as discreditable. This is part of Bauer's general thesis that everywhere and not

[1] H. Lietzmann, *The Beginnings of the Christian Church* (trans. B. L. Woolf, London, 1940), p. 98.

[2] *Rechtgläubigkeit und Ketzerei im ältesten Christentum* (Tübingen, 1934): 2nd edition, ed. Georg Strecker, Tübingen, 1964; cf. especially pp. 49–64. Bauer's theory has become accepted doctrine, cf. for example, R. M. Grant in *The Cambridge History of the Bible* i (Cambridge, 1970), p. 298. For a criticism of his views with particular reference to Antioch, Asia Minor, and Rome see F. W. Norris in *Vigiliae Christianae* 30 (1976), pp. 23 ff., and with reference to Egypt, the present writer's review in *JTS* 16 (1965), pp. 183–5 and a further comment in *American Studies in Papyrology* 1 (New Haven, 1966), pp. 25 ff.

only in Egypt 'heresy' was primary and 'orthodoxy' secondary; if he is right, it is strange that while we know quite a lot about the Church in Asia Minor or Rome we know next to nothing about it in Egypt. General considerations apart, Bauer advances two arguments in support of his theory; firstly, that certain apocryphal works which are closely connected with Egypt are definitely Gnostic in tendency; secondly, and more important, that the only two historical figures of consequence whose names are linked with Egypt before the later second century are both Gnostics, Valentinus and Basilides. The first argument is at best indecisive since e.g. the Gospel according to the Egyptians evinces knowledge of the synoptic gospels and appears to be formally dependent on them; if one circulated in Egypt, in all probability the others did also.[1] And there is no trace as yet in the papyri of the second or third century either of this gospel or of the Gospel according to the Hebrews.

The second argument demands closer scrutiny. Basilides taught in Alexandria in the reign of Hadrian; Valentinus, born in Arsinoe, is recorded as having taught in Rome under Antoninus Pius after a period of activity in Egypt, and we are told that he was trained in Greek culture ($\pi\alpha\iota\delta\epsilon\acute{\iota}\alpha$) in Alexandria![2] The problem here is to some extent one of definition; in the light of Valentinus' career and writings, the dichotomy—either Gnostic or Catholic Christian—however sharp it looked to the experience of later generations, is at this period somewhat unreal. In the early stages of his career he was thought of and seems to have thought of himself as an ordinary or orthodox (if the term can be properly used at this time) Christian; of the Gospel of Truth, coming from his circle and possibly from his pen, A. D. Nock has remarked that it 'was at this time very

---

[1] See M. Hornschuh, *Studien zur Epistula Apostolorum* (*Patristische Texte und Studien*, Bd. 5, Berlin, 1965), pp. 111 ff. and especially n. 49. Hornschuh's view is that the Christian-Gnostic community in Egypt which produced *Gebrauchsliteratur* such as the Gospel according to the Hebrews in the style of the synoptic gospels derived from the original Jewish-Christian community in Palestine for which the life of the historic Jesus was of primary importance. It would follow that the Christians in Egypt were acquainted with the synoptic gospels since the Gnostic texts presuppose non-Gnostic gospels of Palestinian origin. He finds support for his views in the Rylands St. John, in P. Oxy. v. 840 (= H. 585), and in the Egerton Gospel; the origin of the *nomina sacra* suggested in the previous chapter provides still more direct support.

The writer of the *Epistula*, in Hornschuh's opinion, wrote in the first half of the second century, probably in Egypt, and had close connections with Rome; his own Christianity was of a Jewish-Palestinian or synoptic character, differing both from that of the Jewish Christians who depreciated Paul and from that of the Gnostics who claimed Paul for their own interpretation.

His book contains a valuable bibliography on the beginnings of Christianity in Egypt.

[2] For Basilides see Clem. Alex., *Strom.* vii. 106. 4 and Epiphanius, *Haer.* xxiv. 1, p. 686: for Valentinus, Clem. Alex. *Strom.* vii. 17. 106 and Epiphanius, *Haer.* xxxi. 2.

close to the central tradition'.[1] In the next generation or so there was a change; Valentinus' followers, according to Irenaeus,[2] used the four canonical gospels, but while keeping the text changed the meaning; they were criticized not so much for being hostile to the Old Testament as for their arbitrary exegesis of it and for preferring to it their own works. The lines of division are clearly hardening.

There are two further considerations of a more general nature that render Bauer's theory implausible as an explanation of the problem. Even if we accept that in the early second century Christian Gnosticism existed as something quite distinct from Catholic Christianity (in itself improbable), undue weight should not be attached to two individual teachers however important; it would be contrary to what we know of church history elsewhere and at other times if such a Gnosticism flourished alone, provoked by and provoking no contrary movement.[3] While there is no lack of Gnostic texts from Egypt, the manuscripts we have were mostly written in the fourth and fifth centuries when orthodoxy was at the height of its power; one flourished with and stimulated the other. Nor is the literary evidence for Catholic or non-Gnostic Christianity quite so negligible as is sometimes asserted. There is the story in Justin Martyr[4] of the young Alexandrian who applied to the Prefect, L. Munatius Felix, in the year 151/2 for permission to castrate himself; he is described by Justin as τις τῶν ἡμετέρων—'one of ours'—, an expression which either excludes Gnostics or—less probably at this date—includes them in the church catholic.

A more serious objection to this explanation is that it does not explain. Where are the Gnostic papyri of the first two centuries? Unless the movement was strictly confined to Alexandria and the Delta from which no papyri survive, we should expect some manuscript evidence, however slight, to be forthcoming from the papyri. There is one text only, and that ambivalent, from the second century, and both the general cultural relations between Alexandria and the rest of the country and the well-attested presence of Gnosticism in the Arsinoite nome in the reign of Hadrian make a limitation such as that suggested above very improbable. It is significant that before the reign

---

[1] *Essays on Religion and the Ancient World*, ed. Z. Stewart (Oxford, 1972), ii, p. 956.

[2] *Adv. Haer.* iii. 11. 9 (= ii. 52 Harvey).

[3] M. Hornschuh (op. cit., p. 86) sees the author of the *Epistula* together with I Clement and the Pastorals as representing an anti-Gnostic group active in Rome and elsewhere, a group for whom Paul was the *auschlaggebende Autorität*; the Gnostic sect in question may have been that of Basilides.

[4] *Apol.* i. 29.

of Hadrian—the period to which Epiphanius dates the rise of οἱ τὰς αἱρέσεις ἐπινοήσαντες[1]—we know no more of Gnostic than we do of Catholic Christianity; the problem then becomes, not which of the two was predominant, but why there is so little trace of either. The silence of the first hundred years certainly calls for an explanation; but it is not Bauer's.

⌈And once the evidence of the papyri is available, indisputably Gnostic texts are conspicuous by their rarity.⌋ Of the fourteen Christian texts that I would date before A.D. 200[2] there is only one, the first fragment of the Gospel of Thomas from Oxyrhynchus, which may be reasonably be regarded as Gnostic. 'Indisputably Gnostic', since a manuscript of Genesis, for example might have been written by or for either Gnostic or orthodox. Genesis is something of a special case; of more importance than most books of the Old Testament—excepting always the Psalter—to ordinary Christians, it held a peculiar place in the estimation of Gnostics,[3] and was classified by Theodotus among the προφητικαὶ γραφαί.[4] This does not hold of the other books of the Law, and the burden of proof must rest on those who maintain (if any do, for this evidence to the best of my belief has hitherto been ignored) that such early texts of the Old Testament are of Gnostic origin. The Gnostic use of the Old Testament, as R. M. Wilson has remarked,[5] was comparatively restricted; though Deuteronomy and Exodus are cited in the Apocryphon of John and Valentinus says that God spoke through the prophets, what really interested the Gnostics was cosmogony and at times it seems that they knew little of the Old Testament beyond Genesis. Von Campenhausen has pointed out[6] that to judge from the extant fragments Basilides hardly quotes the Old Testament at all while Valentinus' explicit quotations are drawn exclusively from the New Testament. His follower Ptolemaeus in his letter to Flora is concerned not with the Old Testament as a whole but with the Law, and his approach, which allows for different degrees of inspiration

---

[1] *Haer.* xxxi. 2.

[2] See above, pp. 13–14.

[3] Its importance to Gnostic and orthodox alike is reflected both in the frequency with which it occurs in the papyri (see below, p. 61) and elsewhere; thus in the late third or early fourth century a letter of introduction addressed to the priest of Heracleopolis refers to a neophyte as κατηχούμενον ἐν τῇ Γενέσει (P. Oxy. xxxvi. 2785) and from about a century later we have a Coptic treatise taking the form of a dialogue between John and Jesus on the correct interpretation of Genesis as between Gnostic and orthodox (see W. E. Crum in *JTS* (Old Series) xliv (1943), pp. 176 ff.

[4] Clem. Alex. *Excerpta ex Theodoto* 50. 3.

[5] In *Judéo-christianisme . . . Hommages au Cardinal Jean Daniélou* (Paris, 1972), pp. 261 ff.

[6] *The Formation of the Christian Bible* (English translation, J. A. Baker, London, 1972), p. 80.

and value, is intelligently selective, the criterion being provided by the Sayings of the Lord. He may be taken as being representative of the school of Valentinus.

Of the earliest fourteen texts no less than three are of the Psalter, and the Psalter, more used and read than any book of the Old Testament, perhaps more than any book of the Bible, throughout the Christian centuries in Egypt, was as a rule of no particular interest to Gnostics.[1] Another early papyrus, the Chester Beatty Numbers and Deuteronomy, formed part of a collection in which there are no Gnostic texts. If we accept, as I think we must, that manuscripts such as these were written for and used by ordinary Christian communities, their geographical distribution becomes significant; the Bible (to use a slightly anachronistic term) was read in the second century in or near the Arsinoite nome, in the Heracleopolite, in Oxyrhynchus, in Antinopolis. This points to more than a few scattered individuals holding orthodox beliefs and it is the more surprising that the statement can be made today that 'in the second century, as far as our knowledge goes, Christianity in Egypt was exclusively heterodox'.[2]

But if the evidence does not oblige us to accept the view that in Egypt 'heresy' was primary and unchallenged till near the end of the second century, there is much to support Lietzmann's judgement that 'in the second century the Gnostic movement found very fertile soil in Egypt and left a deep mark even on the Church Catholic of Alexandria'.[3] A significant, if small, piece of evidence is that early fragment, to which I have already referred, of Irenaeus' treatise *Adversus Haereses* that reached Oxyrhynchus not long after the ink was dry on the author's manuscript;[4] it testifies both to the orthodox reaction against Gnosticism and to the close relationship between Alexandria and the Church of the West. Further support for this view can be found in the number of Gnostic treatises (with one exception[5] not represented in the papyri of the second and third centuries) thought to have originated in Egypt; the

---

[1] Von Campenhausen, however, points out (op. cit., p. 78) that it was used by them to establish the doctrine of aeons.

[2] R. M. Grant, cf. p. 49, n. 2 above.

[3] Cf. p. 49, n. 1 above.

[4] See above, p. 23.

[5] *The Gospel of Mary* in P. Ryl. iii. 463 (= H. 1065). Other early texts listed by van Haelst under *textes gnostiques* are no. 1060, the so-called 'Psalm of the Naassenes' (on which see Appendix III), and two texts on a Vienna papyrus, nos. 1068 and 1069; of these the first is a fragment of an unknown Hermetic dialogue with no Christian allusions, the second part of the Jewish apocryphon, *The Penitence of Iannes and Iambres* (see below, p. 63).

argument, however, is liable to become circular in that some works are thought to have been written in Egypt because it was the home of Gnosticism and the country's reputation for Gnosticism is enhanced by the existence of these books.[1] It may be noted that a recent study[2] has claimed the anonymous *Epistula Apostolorum* as an Egyptian work of the early second century, representing the views of an orthodox minority in a divided Church, itself dependent on the Jewish Christians of Palestine; given the papyrus evidence, it is interesting that the author of this study finds the epistle both deeply indebted to the Fourth Gospel and ignorant of Pauline theology.

It is possible that the key to what we may call the Gnostic puzzle in second-century Egypt may lie in a passage of Eusebius.[3] In this he tells us that by A.D. 180 Pantaenus, the missionary to India, was in charge of the Catechetical School, adding that 'from ancient custom a school of sacred learning (i.e. of biblical scholarship) had existed in Alexandria'; he further remarks that Pantaenus had been influenced by Stoicism.[4] If Valentinus and Basilides taught in Alexandria, the obvious place for their teaching would have been the School.[5] We know that they held the lead in technical scholarship until the time of Origen; did they perhaps take over the School? It would explain the impact they made, but would not imply that they were dominant throughout the Egyptian Church. And if any system of philosophy is totally opposed in its view of man's place in the universe to the dualist, other-wordly creed of the Gnostics it is that of the Stoics, citizens of the world with a creed of duty to the state and society. Pantaenus' function as head of the School may well have been to cleanse it of Gnostic influence.

To return to the principal problem; why are there so few traces of Egyptian Christianity, Catholic or Gnostic, in any of our sources, literary or documentary, in the first two centuries? We have seen that there may be good reasons for the absence of

---

[1] The Gospel according to the Egyptians must be exempted from this stricture; but to judge from the scanty surviving fragments (not represented among the papyri) the Gospel was encratite but not otherwise heretical (see H. Chadwick, *The Early Church* (London, 1967), p. 64.

[2] See p. 50 n. 1, above.

[3] *H.E.* v. 10.

[4] ἐξ ἀρχαίου ἔθους διδασκαλείου τῶν ἱερῶν λόγων παρ' αὐτοῖς συνεστῶτος. Pantaenus is described as one who ἡγεῖτο τῆς τῶν πιστῶν αὐτόθι (sc. Alexandria) διατριβῆς. On Pantaenus see A. Dihle, *Umstrittene Daten* (Cologne, 1964), pp. 38 and 52.

[5] For the use of Greek philological methods by Basilides and other Gnostics (and also by Papias and Pantaenus) see G. Zuntz, *The Text of the Epistles* (London, 1953), pp. 275–6 and for Pantaenus, p. 273 n. 2.

documentary evidence;[1] but if Christianity had been as active in the first century in Egypt as it was in Ephesus or Corinth, we might expect to find some texts at any rate of the Old Testament from that century and a number larger than in fact we possess of literary texts from the second century, of all centuries the most prolific of literary papyri in general. One fragment, the Yale Genesis, has been ascribed by its editor to the late first century, but it is a dating I should hesitate to accept.[2] If we are forced to conclude that the Church in Egypt in the first century was numerically weak, if not insignificant, the explanation may be found in its relations with Judaism.

For Jews to be on bad terms with their pagan neighbours and for this to result in physical violence was not all that uncommon in the ancient world, but by any standard the situation in Alexandria was exceptional.[3] What was at issue there was not just the size of the Jewish community, important though that was, but its organization.[4] Strabo remarked that a large part of the city was set aside for them, and their ethnarch governed them as though he ruled over an independent state'.[5] When Roman rule began, their possession of a γερουσία gave the Jews a position superior to that of the Greeks in the city. The latter already bitterly resented the demotion of their city from the status of a royal capital to that of the residence of a Roman prefect; that the Jews had from the first taken the Roman side did nothing to improve relations with the Greeks. When in the reign of Claudius—just the time when the Christian mission would be beginning its work—the Jews agitated for the full Alexandrian citizenship, the storm broke.

To chronicle merely the major outbreaks of what were not so much anti-Jewish riots as episodes in an intermittent civil

---

[1] The documentary evidence has been most recently collected by M. Naldini in *Cristianesimo in Egitto* (Florence, 1968); for a detailed review that severely animadverts on Naldini's criteria for admission to the corpus, see E. Wipszycka in *The Journal of Juristic Papyrology*, 18 (1974), pp. 203–21, who accepts no letter or other document earlier than the third century as being unambiguously Christian in reference.

[2] See the references given by van Haelst, op. cit., no. 12. Most recently E. G. Turner in *The Typology of the Early Codex*, p. 19 has ascribed it to the second or third century. I should place it firmly in the second century.

[3] From the abundant literature on the Jewish problem in Egypt in the early Roman period two works may be cited here, both with references to the sources and to recent discussions: P. M. Fraser, *Ptolemaic Alexandria* (Oxford, 1972) i. 54 ff. and 688 ff. with the relevant notes, and the prolegomena by V. Tcherikover to the *Corpus Papyrorum Judaicarum* (Harvard, 1957), pp. 48 ff., whose survey covers the entire period of the papyri.

[4] Fraser (op. cit., i. 688 and ii. 164, n. 315) remarks that the Jewish element in the population of Alexandria was of ever increasing importance from the middle of the second century B.C. down to the early Roman period and he accepts with some reservations Philo's figure (*in Flacc.* 43) of one million for the Jewish population of Egypt.

[5] Quoted by Josephus, *A.J.* xiv. 117.

war between Greeks and Jews: in A.D. 38 on the occasion of a
visit by King Agrippa to Alexandria the ensuing riot resulted in
a large-scale massacre; this was followed in A.D. 41 by an
armed Jewish uprising suppressed by Roman troops with heavy
loss of life; at the beginning of the Jewish war in Palestine
in A.D. 66 the Jews of Alexandria revolted in sympathy and
(according to Josephus) some 50,000 lost their lives. Finally,
there was the disastrous Jewish revolt under Trajan which
spread from Cyrenaica to Egypt and, as we know from the
papyrus documents, led to heavy fighting not only in Alexandria but in Middle and Upper Egypt as well. If we further
remember that the Jewish community in Alexandria, strongly
Hellenized as it was,[1] was more likely than Jewry elsewhere to
give a sympathetic hearing to the Christian mission, it is not
difficult to imagine the situation in which the Christian community found itself. In the early years Christians would be
regarded by pagans as Jews or at most as a Jewish breakaway
movement; if, as we have seen reason to think, Christianity
when it arrived in Egypt had a strongly Jewish stamp, the link
would be all the closer. The internecine feuds between Jews
and Greeks would have constituted a barrier difficult if not
impossible for the Christian mission to surmount. Could a more
unpromising base for the mission to the Greeks than the Delta
quarter of Alexandria be imagined?[2]

The *nomina sacra* are one indication of the strength of Jewish
influence which is borne out by some later evidence.[3] At the
top of a letter written in the middle of the third century from a
Christian in Rome to the church in the Arsinoite nome[4] one
of the recipients copied the opening verses of Genesis in the

---

[1] Fraser (op. cit., ii. 958) observes that there are virtually no Hebrew or Aramaic
inscriptions from Ptolemaic Egypt whereas Greek documents abound.

[2] H. I. Bell in *Cults and Creeds in Graeco-Roman Egypt* (Liverpool, 1953), p. 79 writes: 'Any
Christian community which existed in the city may well have come to a temporary end in the
Jewish revolt under Trajan.' So too J. Daniélou, *History of Early Christian Doctrine*, i (Eng.
trans. London 1964), p. 52 who argues that the Church was immersed in the Jewish colony
and persecuted with it. Christian communities in the χώρα would have been hardly less
affected than that in Alexandria; but a total break in continuity is unlikely.

[3] Eusebius' statement (*H.E.* ii. 16–17) that Christianity spread very rapidly in Alexandria
and that the leading men (ἀποστολικοὶ ἄνδρες) were of Jewish stock who observed most of the
ancient customs in a strictly Jewish fashion must be discounted since it depends on his identification of the first Christian congregation in Alexandria with the Therapeutae. But that the
confusion seemed plausible enough to Eusebius may be regarded as supporting evidence for
the strongly Jewish colouring of early Christianity there. Eusebius' statement is reproduced by Jerome (*De vir. ill.* 8) who gives a further twist to the story (as Dr. J. N. D. Kelly
has pointed out to me) by describing the first Church in Alexandria as *adhuc judaizantem*, a
statement for which there is no independent source.

[4] On this famous letter see most recently H. A. Musurillo in *Chronique d'Égypte* 31 (1956),
pp. 124 ff.

version of Aquila, the strictly literal translation of the Old Testament commissioned by the Jews as an alternative to the Septuagint. And in the early fourth century a woman in Oxyrhynchus alleges in a petition against her husband that he shut the door against her when she went to church, adding that she went to church on the Sabbath;[1] this may be significant in the light of St. Augustine's remark that there would be a riot if a Christian were detected keeping the Jewish Sabbath.[2] We have already noted the popularity in Egypt of *The Shepherd* of Hermas, a work thoroughly Jewish in outlook. Evidence of a different sort may be found in Eusebius' account of the millenarian movement in the Fayûm under Bishop Nepos, successfully and peacefully dealt with by that sympathetic character, Dionysius of Alexandria.[3] We may be pretty sure that Jewish influence in the Church during these centuries was not a recent import but a legacy from an earlier period.[4] Further evidence of the persistence of the Jewish-Christian strain may be discerned in the presence of the apocryphal Epistle of James in the Jung Codex; docetic in character, it is considered to be Jewish-Christian in origin.

The picture that begins to emerge from these different elements is this. In the first age of the Church Christians in Alexandria and consequently throughout Egypt were either unable or unwilling to escape from the Jewish connection, or at any rate to appear to do so in the eyes of non-Christians; the fate of the first church in Alexandria would thus have been involved, willy-nilly, with that of Judaism. There would have been few Gentile converts, and in numbers and influence the

[1] P. Oxy. vi. 903.

[2] *Exp. ep. ad Gal.* 35 (cited by H. Chadwick, *Priscillian of Avila* (Oxford, 1976), p. 75 n. 4).

[3] *H.E.* vii. 24. This passage is cited as evidence of the Jewish character of the Egyptian church by W. H. C. Frend in his essay on *Athanasius as an Egyptian Church Leader* (reprinted in his *Religion Popular and Unpopular in the Early Christian Centuries* (London, 1976), pp. 25 ff.) who also comments that 'Coptic Christianity was to owe more to it [the Jewish-Christian tradition] than to any resurgence of national Egyptian sentiment'. In another paper (*The Gospel of Thomas* in *JTS* xviii (1967), pp. 13 ff.) he has argued for a Christian-Syrian and so Jewish-Christian origin for this gospel, pointing to its emphasis on James and depreciation of Peter; similarly G. Quispel in *Gnosticism and the New Testament* (reprinted in *Gnostic Studies* i (Istanbul 1974), pp. 196 ff.), pp. 252 ff. sees it as Syrian and encratite in character rather than Gnostic. Whether or no this account of the Gospel of Thomas finds acceptance, Frend's explanation of how it made its way up the Nile valley is open to objection. He draws a sharp distinction between the classical Christianity of the School of Alexandria and that of the small towns and later of the countryside, whereas the evidence of the papyri points to close contact between Alexandria and Middle and Upper Egypt and their penetration by Alexandrian scholarship; it is dangerous to assume that because no papyri survive from Alexandria and the Delta Thomas was not read there. And such an argument leaves the riddle of Alexandrian Christianity before Clement unexplained.

[4] M. Hornschuh (see p. 50) also takes the view that the Egyptian Church in its early days was strongly influenced by Judaism, to the extent that the orthodox were in a minority.

church would have remained small. A change in its fortunes
came with the end of the Jewish revolt at the beginning of
Hadrian's reign, and to understand what happened then we
need to look briefly at the further fortunes of Jewry in
Egypt.

Egyptian Jewry survived the war of A.D. 66–70; for the period
between A.D. 70 and 115 there are plenty of documents recorded in the *Corpus Papyrorum Judaicarum* and one or two
literary texts.[1] Because Judaism was a *religio licita* and Jews
after A.D. 70 were subject to the Jewish poll-tax ('Ιουδαϊκὸν
φόρτιον) their documentation is assured; any non-Jewish
Christians would not be distinguished as such by the law and
would remain concealed. The turning point for both communities came with the war under Trajan. This, as the historian
of the Jews in Egypt has remarked, resulted 'in the extermina-
tion of Egyptian Jewry'.[2] From the two hundred and twenty
years between 117 and 337 only forty-four documents with
allusions to Jews are known, a figure that contrasts with nearly
three hundred for the first one hundred and fifty years of
Roman rule. It is precisely when the evidence for Judaism
grows scarce that that for Christianity begins to appear.

For the first time Christians in Egypt were free of the legacy
of their past; in the course of the war they may have been able
to disassociate themselves from the Jews. Both anti-Jewish
Gnostics such as Basilides and the more orthodox Christians
seem to have seized their opportunities. It is to the reign
of Hadrian that Clement of Alexandria dates the beginning
of heresies,[3] while on the other side scholars have seen in
the Epistle of Barnabas the first representative of an Egyptian Christianity that led to Catholicism.[4] Both, though
from very different standpoints, were opposed to orthodox
Judaism.[5]

---

[1] For the literary texts see Appendix I.

[2] V. Tcherikower, op. cit., p. 92.

[3] *Strom.* vii. 106, p. 898 (οἱ τὰς αἱρέσεις ἐπτοηκότες).

[4] Most scholars assign the epistle to the period between A.D. 70 and 100. If we could be
sure that it is Alexandrian in origin, as it is generally considered to be, it would constitute
important evidence on the character of non-Gnostic Christianity in this period; but the
argument rests largely on its allegorizing tendency, and is in some danger of becoming
circular. The earliest allusion to any connection between Barnabas himself and Alexandria
is in Ps.-Clem. i. 9, and lacks any confirmation. L. Goppelt (*Christentum und Judentum in
ersten und zweiten Jahrhundert* (Gütersloh, 1951), pp. 215 ff.) dates the epistle to c. 135, but this
is too late given the tone of the reference to 'the war' (i.e. that of A.D. 66–70) in c. 16. 4.

[5] On the very different attitudes of Barnabas and the Gnostics to the Old Testament see
von Campenhausen, op. cit., p. 70, n. 56; as he observes (n. 52), W. Bauer's attempt to
demonstrate that Barnabas, because it depreciates the historical value of the Old Testament,
is therefore Gnostic is quite unconvincing.

We are not obliged to think that the Christian community came to a temporary end during the war.[1] If Judaism succeeded in maintaining a vestigial existence (as it did), Christianity should not have fared worse; but in this second stage of its life, from A.D. 117 to about 180, there is good reason to think that the Egyptian Church was assisted from without and looked less to Jerusalem and Syria, as it probably had earlier, and more to Rome. Without accepting the hypothesis that the Church of Alexandria was refounded from Rome, we need not doubt that the influence of Rome at this stage was strong; that in the first half of the second century Roman Christianity itself was 'strongly Jewish'[2] would have made its influence all the more acceptable. Contact between Rome and Alexandria was at all times regular and frequent. As far as the Church is concerned, one indication is the presence in the Fayûm in the second century of a fragment of *The Shepherd* of Hermas; another (to which E. R. Hardy has drawn attention[3]) is the close parallel between the parochial organization of Alexandria and that of Rome, while in the late second century the bishops of the two sees regularly exchanged letters on the date of Easter.[4] Conceivably, the use of the codex by Christians in Egypt and the alleged foundation of the Church of Alexandria by St. Mark might be called on in support;[5] but I should hesitate to attach much weight to either for this particular purpose. The case for Roman influence should not be pressed too far. There is a small but telling difference in scribal practice; while, as we have seen, the use of *nomina sacra* is invariable in all Greek manuscripts from the earliest times, in Latin manuscripts, when we first meet them in the fourth century, their use is still far from being regular. Whatever Alexandria got from Rome, it was not its manuscript tradition.

[1] See above, p. 56, n. 2. Still less need we accept H. Lietzmann's statement (op. cit., p. 137: cf. also his *Geschichte der alten Kirche*[2], vol. 3, p. 85) that 'records of a later date [unspecified] furnish grounds for supposing that the capital of Egypt received its Christianity from Rome'. The implausibility of the view that the first Christian mission came from Rome needs no stressing (see above p. 43).

[2] So R. M. Grant in *Gnosticism and Early Christianity* (New York and London, 1966), pp. 122–3, who emphasizes the Jewish character of the theology and moral teaching of Hermas.

[3] *Christian Egypt* (New York, 1952), p. 11.

[4] Ibid., p. 60.

[5] The interpretation of this story, however, whether as fact or legend, is extremely difficult; apart from the silence of Clement and Origen, it is on any showing strange that, if we except the four-gospel Chester Beatty codex, there is no papyrus of the second gospel earlier than the fourth century. Had the legend been promoted by Rome in the second century, some literary allusion or some papyrological evidence might be expected. For the same reason I would now feel even more hesitant about associating the use of the codex for Christian literature with the second gospel than I did when writing *The Codex* (cf. pp. 188–90).

The view has been expressed that in the course of the second century an earlier division between Jewish Christians and Gentile Christians was tending to be replaced by one between Gnostics and Catholics;[1] but from such evidence as we have, the situation seems to have been more fluid and less susceptible of clear definition than this would suggest. As we have observed, the Jewish strain remained strong, and Gnosticism, notwithstanding its hostility to the Old Testament, owed much to Judaism.[2] Some indication of the extent of Gnostic penetration in the second and third centuries may be got from an analysis of what we know to have been read in Egypt. The figures that follow are taken with some modifications from the list of papyri 'antérieures à Constantin' given by von Haelst,[3] and in using them the following considerations should be borne in mind. (i) The figures relate not to manuscripts but to their contents so that a manuscript including more than one work will appear more than once. (ii) Some papyri that may well be Jewish rather than Christian have been included[4] since for this purpose the distinction is not significant. (iii) The Pauline and Johannine epistles are not listed separately with the exception of Hebrews, which has a separate textual history, and the Pastorals, since a codex containing one epistle is very likely to have contained the rest. (iv) As has been mentioned above, there are some texts which may well have been read and owned indifferently by orthodox or Gnostic; the strength of Gnosticism cannot be simply estimated by the ratio of specifically Gnostic books to others, and the striking number of texts both of the Fourth Gospel and of Genesis may well reflect the strength of Gnosticism. (v) The list is one of books and as such does not include the

---

[1] So L. Goppelt (op. cit., p. 213), who sees a landmark in Basilides' activity in Alexandria c. 130; his teaching combined hostility to the Old Testament with docetic tendencies. By dating the Epistle of Barnabas to c. 135, Goppelt has deprived himself of evidence for the earlier existence of Gentile Christianity.

[2] See A. A. T. Ehrhardt in *Studia Evangelica* iii, ed. F. L. Cross (= *Texte und Untersuchungen* 88, Berlin, 1964), pp. 360 ff. He regards the *Epistula Apostolorum* (see above, p. 50) as composed in defence of Jewish Christianity in Egypt c. 180, dependent on the earlier apocryphal Epistle of James, itself of Egyptian origin. While the Jewish Christians contributed significantly to Christian Gnostic literature, he argues (p. 375) that they finally joined the Catholic Church, reluctantly accommodating the system of the *Epistula* to Pauline theology. He observes that the establishment of the celebration of Easter was the lasting contribution of the Jewish Christians to the Church (p. 374).

[3] Op. cit., pp. 409 ff. I have omitted from my analysis nos. 580, 1074, 1076, 1081 (all magical texts which in spite of the occasional use of Jewish or Christian terms there is no need to regard as originated by Christians), 581–2 (Sibylline oracles), 583 (the legend of Ahiqar), 1066 (on which see Appendix III), 674 (Julius Africanus, Κεστοί), and 495 (which I would place in the fourth century and not early in it). I have included no. 592, accidentally omitted from van Haelst's list.

[4] For these see Appendix I.

odd quotation or reminiscence, e.g. the few lines from Genesis written across the letter from Rome or texts written for any purpose on a single sheet or the occasional ostracon.[1] (vi) Though the figures include all papyri probably written before the Peace of the Church, there is no clear cut-off point and a given text may fall one side of the line or the other.

As was to be expected, the Psalter—of not much interest to Gnostics—is represented by more manuscripts than any other book of the Bible, whether of the Old Testament or the New, fourteen in all (though not all would have contained the entire Psalter). Next comes Genesis with nine manuscripts; with the exception of Isaiah and Jeremiah, each present in three manuscripts, no other book of the Old Testament features more than twice, and some—Joshua, Judges, Ruth, 1 and 2 Samuel, 1 and 2 Kings, and Job[2]—do not appear at all, though all with the exception of Ruth are found in later centuries. The Apocrypha is represented only by Wisdom, Ecclesiasticus, and Tobit.

Among New Testament books the frequency of the Fourth Gospel with ten entries is striking, although Matthew with nine[3] runs it close. Luke comes in four manuscripts; what is no less striking than the number of copies of the Fourth Gospel is that the sole text of Mark in our period is that in the Chester Beatty codex of Gospels and Acts.[4] The Gospels have been recorded separately, as not only were the four not a unity at the beginning of our period, but there is evidence for separate circulation. What may be significant is that none of the four is ever found in our period in a 'mixed' codex, that is a codex containing both canonical and non-canonical books. It is curious that often the books which are found in such 'mixed' codices are precisely those whose position in the canon was precarious—the Song of Songs, Ecclesiastes, Wisdom, the Pastorals.[5]

[1] I have also omitted P. Oxy. xxxiv. 2684 (= H. 558), a miniature codex or folded lea with a passage from Jude as it is almost certainly an amulet (see Appendix IV).

[2] Some verses from Job, beginning and ending in the middle of a sentence, were copied out for magical purposes in the early third century in a text that, given its purpose, is remarkably good (BKT. 8. 17 = H. 275, see Appendix IV).

[3] This figure excludes P. Ant. ii. 54 (= H. 347), an amulet or child's booklet containing the Pater Noster in Matthew's version.

[4] That this is not due to the accident of survival can be seen from the Coptic evidence. Th. Lefort has drawn attention in *Muséon* 66 (1953), pp. 16 ff. to some fragments of a Gospel book with extracts from all the Gospels except Mark, and further notes that in Coptic manuscripts of the fourth century there are sixty quotations from Matthew, fifteen from Luke, fifteen from John, and none from Mark.

[5] E. G. Turner, *Typology*, pp. 81–2, gives a list of papyrus codices containing heterogeneous material. All but three of the ten he lists are Christian or contain some Christian texts; they

No longer the (handwritten margin note)

The Pauline Epistles, if we omit Hebrews and the Pastorals, occur in eight manuscripts. Hebrews is found in the Chester Beatty codex of the Pauline Epistles, on the verso of the famous roll of Livy, and in a papyrus codex of the early fourth century.[1] Against this relatively high number must be set the fact that there is as yet no trace of the Paulines in the second century, which may have something to tell us about the early history of the Egyptian Church. The Pastorals occur once only; if we can assume that this manuscript included, besides Titus 1 and 2 Timothy and Philemon, every book of the New Testament is represented, Jude, James, and Revelation each occurring twice, 1 and 2 Peter and the Johannine Epistles once.[2]

Direct evidence of Gnosticism is to be looked for in the non-Biblical texts. In this category there are some seventy papyri within our period; only in one or two cases does one codex carry more than one identifiable work so that the number of separate works is only slightly larger. Those that are specifically Gnostic include three manuscripts of the Gospel of Thomas[3] (which even if encratite rather than Gnostic in origin has unmistakeable Gnostic traits), the Gospel of Mary,[4] and the Wisdom of Jesus Christ.[5] In this category the largest element consists inevitably of unidentified 'theological' texts, mainly small and fragmentary. Two of them are Gnostic;[6] both come from Oxyrhynchus as do the papyri of The Gospel of Thomas, of The Wisdom of Jesus Christ, and possibly that of the Gospel of Mary. But Gnostic works known to us from Coptic translations, from Nag Hammadi or elsewhere or by their

are of interest not only for the history of the Canon but in some cases as providing evidence for the secular reading of Christians. Two certain additions to the list are P. Lit. Lond. 209 + P. Barc. Inv. 84 (see *JTS* 26 (1975), pp. 87–91), a codex (= H. 269) which included the Song of Songs and the Apology of Aristides, and P. Chester Beatty xii which contained besides Melito on the Passion the last chapters of Enoch and the Ezekiel apocryphon (= H. 578, 579, 677). Two possible additions are P. Lond. Inv. 230 and a Vienna papyrus. The first consists of P. Lit. Lond. 207 (= H. 109) and 255, having Psalm 11 (12), 7–14 (15) 4 on one side and a passage from Isocrates *Ad Demonicum* on the other; both were used as reading or shorthand exercises, and it is uncertain whether the manuscript was a codex or an opistho-graph roll. The second, more likely perhaps to be part of a roll than of a codex, is P. Vindob. Graec. 29828 and 29456 (= H. 1068), the latter being not a Gnostic text but part of *The Peni-tence of Iannes and Iambres*, while the former carries an unknown Hermetic text. (Neither was correctly identified by their first editor H. Oellacher in his publication in *Miscellanea G. Galbiati* 2 (Milan, 1951), pp. 182–8.) Opisthograph rolls such as that with the Livy Epitome on one side and Hebrews on the other are a less reliable index of Christian reading since the possibility that an already written roll was purchased and reused has to be borne in mind.

[1] P. Oxy. viii. 1078 = H. 539.

[2] There is also a Coptic text of 1 Peter in the Mississippi Paschal codex (see below, p. 68), falling within our period.

[3] = H. 593, 594, 595.

[4] = H. 1065.   [5] = H. 1064.   [6] = H. 1070 and 1151.

titles from orthodox opponents such as Epiphanius or Irenaeus are conspicuously absent from the list. It may be no coincidence that the Treatise on the Passion of Melito of Sardis, a champion of orthodoxy, occurs in three Greek and two Coptic manuscripts within or just after our period.[1] One other papyrus in this somewhat miscellaneous category should be mentioned here, an anthology of prayers now in Berlin, in character Gnostic and syncretistic;[2] together with some Christian prayers is the final hymn of Poimandres from the Hermetic corpus. In one of the Christian prayers the *nomina sacra* are used, while in another they are not; the degree to which they are observed or neglected may be a criterion of the attachment or the reverse of a Gnostic sect to Christianity.

Outside the Bible the most widely-read book was *The Shepherd* of Hermas; it is found in seven manuscripts, and its popularity is evidence both of the continuing Jewish-Christian strain in Egypt and of the link between Rome and Alexandria. There are five or six fragments of apocryphal gospels (with small fragments the distinction between a gospel and a commentary is not always clear), three texts of that popular romance, the Acts of Paul, three texts attributed to Origen, one of them contemporary or all but contemporary. What impresses most is the range of reading among educated Christians in provincial Egypt; apart from the authors already mentioned, we find Philo, Clement of Alexandria, Barnabas, Aristides, Julius Africanus, not to mention such works of popular piety as the Protevangelium of James and *The Penitence of Iannes and Iambres,* the two magicians who competed unsuccessfully with Moses.[3] There is nothing provincial or narrowly pietist about such a list; it matches the wide range of secular literature read in the towns and villages of Egypt.

We have noted that the early texts of Melito include two in Coptic, one of which is plausibly assigned on palaeographical grounds to the third century. This prompts the questions both how far within our period the mission to the

---

[1] The Greek texts are H. 677–9; the two Coptic texts are that in the Mississippi codex, ed. W. H. Willis (ascribed by him to the third century) and a fragment published (but not at that time identified) in W. E. Crum and H. I. Bell, *Wadi Sarga* (= *Coptica* iii, Copenhagen, 1922) no. 17, pp. 47–9, possibly fourth century in date. Two other papyri within our period have been doubtfully assigned to other works of Melito (H. 681–2) and a third (H. 680) dated to the fifth century.

[2] H. 722.

[3] The identification of a substantial fragment of this work on a papyrus now in Toronto has been announced by A. Pietersma; the text on the recto of the Vienna papyrus referred to above (p. 62) has now been identified and republished by P. Maraval in *ZPE* 25 (1977) pp. 199 ff.

Copts was taken by the Church, which hitherto has presented itself as a purely Greek institution and, following on that, how influential Gnosticism was among the Copts.[1] If the view held by some scholars is accepted, that the Gnostics anticipated the Catholics in their appeal to the native Egyptians and that early Coptic literature is predominantly Gnostic in character, this would substantially modify our estimate of the nature of the Egyptian Church. This is territory in which anyone who is not a Coptic scholar must move warily, the more so in view of the important discoveries of Coptic manuscripts in recent years, many of them as yet unpublished; but in as far as conclusions depend on the dates assigned to manuscripts the Greek palaeographer has some *locus standi* since Coptic palaeography in this period is essentially derivative from Greek.[2] We have to allow for the possibility that a Coptic scribe may on occasion have taken an older rather than a contemporary Greek manuscript as his model;[3] I have therefore been conservative in admitting Coptic texts to the list of manuscripts prior to the early fourth century.

While it is generally agreed that almost the entire New Testament and much of the Old Testament existed in the Sahidic dialect before at latest the end of the fourth century and that translations into other dialects were being made, how far back the translations reached and what was the relation of Sahidic to other dialects is very much a matter of debate among experts.[4] The history of Christianity in the Coptic tongue before

---

[1] It is difficult, if not impossible, to form an estimate however rough of the proportion of the population in the Roman period whose sole language was Egyptian whether it took the written form of Demotic or later of Coptic. Much work has been done on the ἀγράμματοι, those who could not read or write Greek: see H. C. Youtie in *Harvard Studies in Classical Philology* 75 (1971), pp. 163 ff. (reprinted in *Scriptiunculae* ii, p. 612) and the same writer in *ZPE* 19 (1975), pp. 101 ff. and ibid., pp. 201 ff. There can be little doubt that Youtie is correct when he writes that 'the language of the native population remained Egyptian . . . up to and beyond the Arab conquest'. Some of them may have understood a little Greek though they could not write or read it; but the easy understanding of the Gospels and on the part of a few at least the ability to copy them and read from them was a necessary precondition for the success of any missionary effort. Hence, as Youtie points out, for the first time Greek literature—not classical literature but the Greek Bible—was translated into the Egyptian language.

[2] On this point see R. Kasser, *Les Origines du christianisme égyptien* in *Rev. de Théol. et de Phil.* 12 (1962), pp. 15 ff.

[3] A good example is provided by the Coptic letters published in P. Jews and datable within narrow limits and the abundant Greek hands of the same period.

[4] See G. Mink, *Die koptischen Versionen des N.T.* in *Die alten Übersetzungen des N.T., die Kirchenväterzitate und Lektionäre*, ed. K. Aland (Berlin–New York, 1972), pp. 160 ff. and especially pp. 181 ff. Mink convincingly controverts two theses of Kasser's—that Sahidic was the dialect of Alexandria and that the Sahidic version of the Bible achieved 'canonical' status *c.* A.D. 300, translations into other dialects being made from it. Mink considers that the development of Coptic writing and literature came with the Peace of the Church, receiving a profound stimulus from the monastic movement.

A.D. 300 is obscure; but there are a few patches of light worth inspection.

The first indications that Christianity had spread to the native population are found in the third century. Origen is the first to talk of Christian Αἰγύπτιοι as distinct from Ἕλληνες;[1] but when Eusebius states that in the persecution of Septimius Severus at the very beginning of the third century martyrs came 'from Egypt and the whole Thebaid',[2] they are unlikely to have been all Greek-speakers. It is clear from his account that the church grew apace under the great bishop Dionysius (247–64) and a letter of Dionysius that he quotes mentions 'Egyptians' (as well as Libyans) martyred in Alexandria under Decius.[3] In the last quarter of the century St. Antony, who never learned Greek, heard the lessons being read in church;[4] whether from a Coptic manuscript or from oral translation we do not know. (Wherever there were Egyptian Christians the lessons would have been translated for them into whatever dialect they spoke; hence the variety of early written Coptic dialects.)

In a papyrus from Oxyrhynchus of February 304 one Aurelius Ammonius, *lector* of the former village church of Chusis, states that the church had nothing of value—gold, vestments, flocks, land—except for the bronze gates already removed to Alexandria;[5] he himself, although a *lector*, is described in the document as not knowing letters (μὴ εἰδὼς γράμματα). In other words, he did not know Greek and must have read the lessons to his flock in Coptic. Diocletian's edict of 303 had ordered the total destruction of churches; hence the reference to the 'former' church.

It is at just this time we hear of the first Coptic scholar and teacher known to us.[6] Hieracas, who wrote in Greek as well as

[1] See Harnack, op. cit., p. 725 n. 1. The precise meaning to be given to the term Αἰγύπτιοι is not clear; it most probably denotes those excluded from the privileged class in the nome capitals, the metropolites or οἱ ἀπὸ γυμνασίου. It does not necessarily imply an inability to understand Greek. Because some of the confessors of the persecution under Decius bore Egyptian names—Horus, Ater, Isidorus, Nemesion—it is very far from meaning, as the documentary papyri show, that they cannot have known Greek. This situation is misinterpreted by Kasser, loc. cit., pp. 11 and 22.

[2] *H.E.* vi. 1.

[3] Ibid., vi. 41. 19. As Bell points out (*Cults and Creeds in Graeco-Roman Egypt*, p. 88) the fact that Dionysius describes three or four of the confessors as 'Egyptians' suggests that the Egyptian element as compared with the Greek was still small.

[4] Athanasius, *Vita Antoni*, 1. 2.

[5] P. Oxy. xxxiii. 2673; the document was drafted on his behalf by Aurelius Serenus.

[6] He may have had a predecessor in Paul the Anchorite who, according to *The Paradise of the Fathers* i, p. 198, in the time of Decius was 'educated in the learning of the Greeks and Egyptians', if Paul was not an entirely mythical figure (cf. J. D. N. Kelly, *St. Jerome* (London, 1975), index s.v. Paul).

in Coptic, had been trained in both Greek and Egyptian sciences—medicine, astronomy, and magic—and in addition was a good biblical scholar.[1] There can be no doubt that up till now Egyptian Christianity had been predominantly Greek,[2] and it has often been said that the change came with the monks.[3] In fact, it came earlier; while the early anchorites and, still more, the first monasteries in the early fourth century exercised an immense attractive power, the foundations of Coptic Christianity had already been laid, and the first monks must have been trained and taught by Hieracas and men like him. None the less, well beyond the period with which we are concerned, the Greek Bible remained the only authoritative text.

Probably the earliest manuscript evidence for the mission to the Copts is a Graeco-Coptic glossary to Hosea and Amos written on the back of a land register and datable to the late third century.[4] Each column deals with twenty verses of text, the Greek first, sometimes abbreviated, then the Coptic, always in full. The same hand, described by the editor as an 'educated cursive' (the hand of a private scholar), wrote both; the dialect is Middle Egyptian and represents an early stage in the development of Coptic. It is likely to have been written by a teacher for his class of catechumens; the editors think of this as taking place in a monastery, but at this date the *mise-en-scène* would have been the local church school.

From much the same time come the glosses in Old Fayûmic (Coptic written without the seven additional letters) in the margin of the Chester Beatty Isaiah[5] and, not much later, the Sahidic glosses in the Freer codex of the Minor Prophets.[6] We now find Copts, more familiar with their native language than with Greek, engaged in writing Greek manuscripts; the editor of the Chester Beatty Melito pointed out[7] that on page 17 the scribe wrote $\rho\iota\tau\iota$ where he should have put $\rho\iota\psi$, one form of ψ being in Coptic the symbol for $\tau\iota$.[8]

---

[1] Epiphanius, *Haer.* lxvii. 1. 2–3 (= Holl iii. 133).

[2] H. Delehaye, *Les Martyrs d'Égypte* (Brussels, 1923), p. 30 has commented that three-quarters of the names of the Egyptian martyrs under Diocletian are Greek; while the bearer of an Egyptian name may have been Greek-speaking, Greek martyrs are more likely to have been conspicuous and so remembered than Egyptian peasants.

[3] G. Bardy in *Memorial Lagrange* (Paris, 1940), pp. 203 ff. His view of the early church in Egypt is peculiar and needs severe qualification; thus he considers (p. 206) that by the time of Origen Christianity had not reached beyond Alexandria and, more strange still, that Greek was unknown in Upper Egypt (p. 207).

[4] See H. I. Bell–H. Thompson in *JEA* 11 (1925), pp. 241–6.

[5] = H. 293.   [6] = H. 284.   [7] = H. 677.

[8] We may compare the Jude (= H. 557) and 1 and 2 Peter (= H. 548) in the Bodmer composite codex of the fourth century (for the date see now E. G. Turner, *Typology*,

There are a number of Coptic manuscripts that may reasonably be regarded as having been written within our period; any conclusions drawn from the composition of the list must allow for the chances of survival, as the rule of Pachomius, the founder of monasticism, may serve to remind us. This was drawn up in A.D. 321 and certainly assumes that Psalter and Gospels, the reading of which was obligatory on postulants, were available in Coptic; yet no Coptic gospel datable within our period has yet been discovered. Among the earliest are an Ecclesiastes in Louvain of the late third or early fourth century, described as being 'in a professional calligraphic hand from a scriptorium equally used to Greek and Coptic'[1] and a Melito which Professor Kasser would regard as being one of the two oldest Coptic manuscripts, the other being the codex of Proverbs in the Bodmer collection.[2] Coeval with these and (in the late Dr. Kahle's judgement) 'the earliest witness of the standard Sahidic version of any part of the Bible', is a bilingual book in the form of a school tablet.[3] H. I. Bell had noted that the teacher's hand on this tablet was that of the Greek cursive of the third or fourth century and its latest editor ascribes it to the later third century. Together with arithmetical tables and paradigms it has a paraphrase in Greek of the opening lines of *Iliad* i and eight verses of Psalm 46 in Coptic; the writer was a Christian whose first language was Greek. A school exercise book of slightly later date in the Bohairic dialect has verses—perhaps written down from memory—from Job, St. John's Gospel, and Romans.[4]

There are two other manuscripts I should place in the same group.[5] The first is a bilingual codex in Hamburg which

---

pp. 79–80). There is a Coptic note on 2 Peter and the confusion in the Greek between κ and γ is said by the editor to be characteristic of the Copts of Thebes; the way in which the scribe places a diaeresis on an iota suggests an imperfect knowledge of Greek.

[1] Th. Lefort, *Les Manuscrits coptes de l'Université de Louvain*, no. 9, pp. 60 ff., pl. v. The editor compares the hand to that of P. Oxy. ix. 1179, ascribed to the second/third century; the *tau* resembles that in P. Oxy. vii. 1016 of the third century. Cf. also P. Kahle in *Bala'izah* (London, 1954), p. 238.

[2] See R. Kasser, *L'Évangile de S. Jean* (Neuchâtel, 1966), pp. 7 ff.

[3] Bodleian, Gr. Inscr. 3019. The Coptic text was edited by W. E. Crum in *Mémorial Lagrange*, who quotes Bell's verdict on the date, cf. also Kahle, op. cit., p. 237; it has now been fully edited by P. J. Parsons, *A School Book in the Sayce Collection* in *ZPE* 6 (1970), pp. 133 ff. whose interpretation I follow.

[4] See E. M. Husselman in *Journal of the Near Eastern Society* 6 (1949), pp. 129 ff., who quotes H. I. Bell's view that the teacher's hand resembles that of Greek cursive of the third/fourth century; cf. also Kahle, op. cit., p. 251. The early date has been queried by A. Vööbus, *Early Versions of the New Testament* (Stockholm, 1954), p. 232.

[5] Other texts which Kahle places in the first half of the fourth century include the codex of Deuteronomy Jonah and Acts in the British Library, published by A. E. Wallis Budge, *Coptic Biblical Texts* (London, 1912). Kenyon (quoted by Budge) assigned this to the first

together with the Acts of Paul in Greek contains the Song of Songs and Lamentations in Old Fayûmic, an unidentified work, and Ecclesiastes in both Greek and Coptic;[1] it was probably written about the year 300. The second is an exceptionally interesting manuscript, the Crosby Codex i in Mississippi. This professionally written volume contains Melito on the Passion, the story of the Maccabean martyrs—the prototypes of all Christian martyrs—from Second Maccabees, the first Epistle of Peter, Jonah, and a contemporary Easter homily, all in Sahidic.[2] (As Dr. Willis, its editor, remarks, it was throughout Paschal in character and may have been a lector's book for a pre-Nicene celebration of Easter.) It has plausibly been dated to the third century, and the comment may be made that if books such as this were available in Coptic, they must surely have been preceded by translations of Genesis, the Psalter, and the Gospels. It is remarkable, too, that this Easter anthology contains no excerpt from the Gospels, in conformity with the apparent rule that they were not included in mixed codices. Throughout this group the presence, naturally enough, of teaching texts, for adults perhaps rather than for children, and in conformity with this a preference for sententious works such as Proverbs or Ecclesiastes are noteworthy.

'The Gnostics were the first to have grasped the importance of preaching in the native language'; so Professor Bardy writing in 1940.[3] No doubt Coptic was employed for an oral translation of the lessons in church before they were put in written form, and maybe for other purposes; but I have been unable to discover any evidence that the Gnostics ever preached in Coptic within our period. That towards the end of this period certain books were translated into Coptic is, as we have seen, quite certain; had these books been unmistakeably Gnostic in character and if the Gnostics, not the orthodox, were responsible for the translation of the Bible, in other words if they were the pacemakers of the conversion of the native population, that would be convincing testimony to the predominance of Gnosticism in Egyptian Christianity.

half of the third century, arguing from the resemblance of some cursive prayers in Coptic at the end of Acts to the contemporary Greek documentary style; but the main hand with its strongly vertical inclination points to the fourth century. Turner, *Typology*, p. 137 dates it to 330/350. Other texts placed by Kahle, op. cit., p. 203 in this period are the Berlin Genesis, the Ascension of Isaiah and a manuscript of psalms or hymns.

[1] The Greek texts are H. 605 and 263; for the Coptic see Kahle, op. cit., pp. 227 ff.
[2] See W. H. Willis in *Proc. IX Int. Congress Papyrology*, pp. 383 ff. Turner, *Typology*, p. 137 ascribes it to the third or fourth century.
[3] *Mémorial Lagrange*, p. 207.

Professor Bardy's views have been echoed more recently both by Dr. R. Kasser who writes that 'literary Coptic begins with heterodox sects (Gnostics); their proselytizing enthusiasm drove the orthodox into similar campaigns'[1] and by Professor A. Vööbus according to whom 'the earliest type of Christianity among the Coptic-speaking population was Gnostic'.[2] On the face of it, it would be strange if a strongly intellectualist movement had a greater appeal to the native population than orthodoxy, particularly if, as we have seen reason to think, it had not in the third century won a dominant position among the Greeks, surely much more open to its attractions. Gnostic texts were, of course, circulating in Greek in the third century in the Egyptian towns—we need only think of the Gospel of Mary and the Wisdom of Jesus Christ—and since it still has to be demonstrated that any original Gnostic works were composed in Coptic, Greek must have been the medium by which they first made their impact. The attraction of Gnosticism for the Copts in the late fourth and fifth centuries is manifest in the surviving manuscripts of which the Nag Hammadi and the Manichaean codices are the most conspicuous; but there is no clear reason for antedating it.

If these statements I have quoted were correct, we should expect to find that the Gnostic and Manichaean manuscripts in Coptic antedated the earliest Coptic manuscripts of the Bible for which there is no reason to posit a Gnostic background; but this is not the case. If we examine the contents of the manuscripts which can be dated to about A.D. 300, a few of them being earlier, we get the following list of books extant in Coptic or which can safely be assumed to have been extant:

Hosea and Amos (glossary)
Isaiah (glossary)
Minor Prophets (glossary)
Ecclesiastes (two manuscripts)
Psalm 42
Song of Songs
Lamentations
Jonah
2 Maccabees
1 Peter
Melito on the Passion

---

[1] See above, p. 64, n. 2. He observes, however, that Gnostic manuscripts in Coptic are not older than the Biblical ones; this hardly squares with the hypothesis of a Gnostic missionary campaign anticipating that of the orthodox.   [2] Op. cit., p. 215.

Melito (an unknown work)
Paschal Homily

If the school tablet in Bohairic, referred to above, is included,[1]
Job, the Fourth Gospel, and Romans should be added to the list.
Melito was a combatively orthodox bishop; the Gnostics had
little interest in most books of the Old Testament; can we really
detect in this list the hand of a vigorous and propagandist
Gnostic movement? The equation Coptic = Gnostic is in this
period very far from being true.

If we take a somewhat wider view, the result is not all
that different. The late P. E. Kahle in his invaluable study of
Der Bala'izah, published in 1954, gives an analysis by format,
dialect, and content of all Coptic manuscripts prior to the
sixth century.[2] Of 163 manuscripts, 34 are of the Old Testament
or the canonical Apocrypha, exclusive of the Psalter, 17 of the
Psalter, 56 of the New Testament, 5 of the Old Testament
Apocrypha, 9 each of the New Testament apocrypha and the
fathers, 19 are Gnostic, 7 Manichaean, 7 are fragments whose
contents are unidentified. Even when allowance is made for a
few of the Old Testament manuscripts and some of the New
Testament and apocryphal texts being of Gnostic origin, the
story they tell is clear enough. If Professor Vööbus is correct
in saying (and it seems a somewhat sweeping statement) that
Gnostic Christianity was not interested in the texts of Catholics,
that is in the New Testament, then it becomes impossible to
accept his view of the position of Gnosticism in Coptic Christianity.

Kahle's analysis brings to light another interesting fact.
There is a quite remarkable predominance of Gnostic texts,
mostly of the fourth, some of the fifth century in the sub-
Achmimic dialect; the only exceptions are a fourth century
Gospel of John, a Hebrews possibly of the same century,
and a fifth century Acts of Paul. Panopolis then may have been
a centre of Gnosticism analogous to whatever centre further
south preserved the Nag Hammadi codices and contrasting perhaps with Oxyrhynchus. The author of the *Historia Monachorum
in Aegypto* describes Oxyrhynchus as a very large city active in
works of charity and hospitality: there were twelve churches,
five thousand monks in monasteries within the city and another
five thousand in those without: no pagans, no heretics, more
monks than laymen.[3] The picture is highly idealized and the

[1] See above, p. 67.   [2] Op. cit., pp. 269 ff.
[3] Ed. A. J. Festugière, *Subsidia Hagiographica* 34 (1960), 5 .1.

numbers, except perhaps that for the churches, are only of rhetorical significance (cf. the author's figure of twenty thousand virgins), but Oxyrhynchus at this time may well have been more of an orthodox Christian centre than other cities.[1] We know that pagan practices and pagan cultural life lingered longer at Panopolis than elsewhere; that Gnosticism also flourished there points to the natural link between it and Greek rather than Egyptian culture. The contrast between the two may serve as a warning against hasty generalizations and as a reminder that conditions varied from area to area.

From this standpoint we may take a backward glance at the early history of the Church in Egypt in as far as we can piece it together from a variety of sources, admittedly often fragmentary and none as informative as we could wish; future discoveries may change the perspective. The original Christian mission to Egypt, addressed to the Jews and particularly to the Jews of Alexandria, came from the Church in Jerusalem. This mission miscarried, its task becoming increasingly difficult as relations between Jews and Greeks and Jews and Romans became exacerbated; it was closely identified with Judaism, all the more so because the gospel that reached Egypt was Jewish in emphasis rather than Pauline. It persisted, however, and spread slowly and a tradition of scholarship, once established in the favourable soil of Alexandria, took root early and may well have had an unbroken existence up to the time of its flowering at the end of the second century. Then, when the link with Judaism was snapped in the twenties of the second century, the suppressed energies of the church found expression in a variety of directions. We may surmise that for much of the second century it was a church with no strong central authority and little organization; one of the directions in which it developed was certainly Gnosticism, but a Gnosticism not initially separated from the rest of the Church. It was the teaching and personality of the two Gnostic leaders, Basilides and Valentinus, that impressed the Christian world outside Egypt and were remembered, but this was not the whole story. As the second century went on, Roman influence grew, all the more readily as the foundations of both churches had been laid not by Paul, but indirectly at least in the case of Alexandria by the apostles from Jerusalem. Gradually, too, under Roman influence the line between Gnostic and Catholic Christianity

---

[1] Antinoë was still largely pagan when Theodoret visited it in A.D. 372; cf. his *Hist. Eccl.* iv. 18. 7–14.

was more sharply drawn; but in Egypt, as can be seen in
Clement and Origen, the process was slow and distinctions
sometimes remained blurred. But thanks perhaps to Rome and
certainly to the Catechetical School of Alexandria as reformed
under Pantaenus the Church grew both in numbers and
organization and by the end of the century was ready to ad-
vance. At this point the mission to the Copts begins.

We have already had occasion to note[1] the statement by
Professor R. M. Grant that 'in the second century, as far as
our knowledge goes, Christianity in Egypt was exclusively
"heterodox" ', and have seen reason to think that this view
which goes back to Bauer's theory of the origins of the Egyptian
Church is mistaken. The picture as we have found it turns out to
be remarkably like that described by Professor Grant elsewhere
in the same essay. Here he gives a description of what he calls
'common core Christianity' in the second century, defined by its
rejection of docetism, its acceptance of the Old Testament, and
the belief that the revelation was available to all, not just
to a spiritual élite. He goes on to point out that this 'embryonic orthodoxy [was] related to a common core of books
accepted by most Christians', Gnostics included, and that the
presupposition for the beginning of a canon of Scripture is a
'relatively fixed norm of faith expressed by the acceptance of
books regarded as authoritative'.[2] If we consider what might be
called the reading list of the provincial Church in Egypt in the
second century with its stress on the Old Testament, the absence
of any docetic texts, and the rarity of any specifically Gnostic
ones and if we further remember the theology implicit in the
nomina sacra, we shall find that the Church in Egypt answers
remarkably well to Professor Grant's definition. It may have
been somewhat indiscriminate in what it admitted, whether by
way of Jewish practices and beliefs or by way of Gnosticism
and it may not have been highly organized; it was a church
diverse but with a degree of unity in its diversity, growing
healthily in a way that does not admit of any one label being
easily attached to it: in fact a normal church of its time in
which wheat and tares (from an orthodox standpoint) grew
together to harvest.

Such a development helps to explain the sudden flowering of
the Church in the fourth century; the seed had been well sown
in the first and second centuries and the plant well tended in the
third. From the second quarter of the fourth century onwards

¹ See above, p. 53.   ² Op. cit., p. 286; cf. also p. 296.

Egyptian Christianity comes into the full light of day; drawing on the resources of Egyptian nationalism (for in Christianity, as H. I. Bell has written, 'for the first time since the third century B.C. the very soul of Egypt found unfettered expression')[1] it gained enormous impetus and became the inspiration and teacher of the Christian world. At that point we take leave of it.

[1] *Egypt from Alexander the Great to the Arab Conquest* (Oxford, 1948), p. 113.

APPENDICES

I. *Jewish theological papyri of the Roman period*

From time to time various papyri of the Old Testament have been claimed for Judaism rather than for Christianity, e.g. P. Oxy. iv. 656 (= H. 13) and P. Oxy. vii. 1007 (= H. 5), but to the best of my knowledge the only full discussion of the criteria to be applied is that by K. Treu in *Kairos* 15 (1973), pp. 138 ff. He correctly observes that in crediting such papyri to Christians rather than to Jews three tests have usually been employed:

(a) the use of the LXX on the ground that from the second century onwards this fell into disfavour with Jews in consequence of its adoption by Christians as the standard Biblical text;

(b) the use of the codex instead of the roll;

(c) the use of *nomina sacra*.

He regards none of these as a foolproof criterion.

On the first he observes that, while the LXX was certainly exposed to adverse comment by Jews in the Christian era and while the more literal translation of Aquila, definitely Jewish in origin and intended to replace the LXX, was publicly endorsed by leading Rabbis, yet the LXX was still used and used officially in synagogues; the attitude to it was ambivalent. On the second he points out that, while the use of skin was prescribed for the Torah and while the roll remained the only approved format for liturgical purposes, yet papyrus was frequently used instead of skin and there was no reason why for private study a Jew should not read the scriptures in a codex—one of many accommodations to the ways of the non-Jewish world. As for the third criterion, Treu takes it for granted that the contraction and overlining of θεός and κύριος is of Jewish origin, citing in support only P. Oxy. vii. 1007. He also very justly notes that Christians had access to Jewish manuscripts, witness the work of Origen, and the not infrequent assumption of editors that a given Christian text of the Old Testament was copied from a Jewish original; it would be a mistake to think that there was not frequent contact between Jews and Christians (especially, we may add, given the strongly Jewish character of much of Egyptian Christianity). He lists some sixteen papyri of the Old Testament that in the light of his observations might as well be Jewish as Christian, and concludes that there are more Jewish biblical papyri of the Roman period than has generally been allowed, and that the evidence, documentary as well as literary, points to a long and close association between Jews and Christians.

Before examining these criticisms of the criteria usually applied it may be worth observing that from the Ptolemaic period when the

Jewish community in Egypt was important and thriving in a way that contrasts with its fortunes through most of the Roman period only two biblical papyri survive, P. Ryl. iii. 458 (= H. 57) and P. Fouad Inv. 266 (= H. 56). It is true that there are far fewer literary papyri in general surviving from the Ptolemaic era, but none the less this small figure may serve as a warning against ascribing too many Old Testament papyri of the Roman period to the diminishing Jewish community; it has too to be remembered that Jewish reverence for the name of God may well have led them to have been much more careful about disposing of worn-out or unwanted manuscripts than were Christians with not the same feeling about the sacredness of a piece of papyrus or parchment carrying the divine name. Again, the contrast between the plain, quasi-documentary hand of the earliest Christian papyri and the formal elegance of Jewish manuscripts may reflect the difference between the legally protected synagogue with its *Torahschrein* and the house-church of an unrecognized association.

It is, I believe, practicable to give greater precision to the criteria listed and criticized by Treu. If we consider first the character of the text, we must agree that in any given text the use of the LXX from the second century onwards does not by itself exclude a Jewish origin. On the other hand, not only was the Jewish attitude to this version ambivalent, but the one sacred and authoritative text for Jews was the Hebrew, and the more Judaism turned its back on the Greek world after the disasters of the first half of the second century, the more Hebrew reasserted its place in the synagogue against Greek.[1] For Christians, on the other hand, the LXX was the recognized and standard text; it was not replaced, as to a large extent it was for those Jews who still used a Greek translation, by other versions, especially that of Aquila. Consequently, where no other factors are present, there is a presumption that a manuscript of the LXX from the second century onwards is more likely to be Christian than Jewish; where, however, the text departs markedly from the *textus receptus* thus pointing to a revised version, this could be an indication of Jewish origin. Conversely, a manuscript carrying the version of Aquila is more likely to be Jewish than Christian.[2]

Secondly, Treu's contention that the codex might be used in place of the roll by Jews for private study, and that therefore it does not constitute evidence of Christian origin, should be accepted only with some reservations. For though the Jews in later times accommodated themselves on occasion to Christian or pagan practice and deserted the roll for the codex, that they used it regularly in the second century,

---

[1] The editors of the *Corpus Papyrorum Judaicarum* (vol. i, p. 94) in their prolegomena write that 'the general impression is that of a complete breakdown of Jewish life in Egypt, at any rate at the beginning of this period' (*sc.* A.D. 117–337). On the replacement of Greek by Hebrew in Jewish life see ibid., pp. 101–2 and 107.

[2] An exception is P. Amh. i. 3 (c) (= H. 3), the first five lines of Genesis in the version of Aquila as well as in that of the LXX; they are written on the verso of a Christian letter.

still more that they originated it, is highly improbable. The evidence that Christians used the codex for both the Old and New Testaments from the earliest times is indisputable, so much so that we do not know of any copy of any of the Gospels written on a roll;[1] there is no comparable evidence for its use in the second and third centuries by Jews. Consequently, other factors being equal, there is a reasonable assumption that a text of the Old Testament in codex form is more likely to be Christian than Jewish. The converse again holds; such a text on a roll is, prima facie, to be regarded as Jewish in origin.

We have seen reason above[2] to believe that the contractions of θεός and κύριος—the only *nomina sacra* really relevant in this context— are a Christian, not a Jewish invention, and we should not therefore expect to find them in any manuscript written by a Jew for Jews. But, as Treu has observed, it is a mistake to think of Jews as an entirely enclosed community unaffected by the practices of the pagan or indeed the Christian world surrounding them. We have already noticed[3] in a Jewish manuscript of the sixth century one or two instances of the contraction of κύριος where pressure of space made it convenient, contrasting with many instances of the uncontracted form in the same manuscript; naturally enough, the scribe was well aware of the prevailing usage. It would not be surprising were one or two instances to be found in an earlier period; but they will certainly be the exceptions, not the rule.

Very tentatively it may be suggested that there is a fourth criterion, to be applied only in association with one or all of the others, and that is the character of the script. There seems to have been a distinctive style of writing used for Jewish copies of the scriptures in Greek from the second century B.C. onwards and still used, with modifications of course, down to the third century A.D.;[4] a parallel would be the development of the so-called Biblical Uncial or Biblical Majuscule, familiar from but by no means limited to the great Biblical codices and their predecessors among the papyri. But not all Greek manuscripts known to be Jewish are written in this style, witness the roll of the Minor Prophets from Engedi (= H. 285), and parallels to it can be found among the secular literary papyri.

If then we use these revised criteria, the following texts of the Old Testament of Egyptian provenance and assigned to the Roman period should most probably be regarded as Jewish:

(1) P. Oxy. iv. 656 (= H. 13), a papyrus codex of Genesis assigned to the second century.[5] There are no abbreviations of *nomina sacra*; where the Tetragrammaton should be written the first scribe left a

---

[1] And none of any book of the New Testament on the *recto* of a roll: see above, p. 23.

[2] See above, pp. 29 ff.　　　　　　　　　　　　　　　　　　　[3] See above, pp. 32–3.

[4] The style of these Jewish manuscripts needs closer examination and definition than they have as yet been given, especially in the use of serifs (for these see *GMAW*, p. 25).

[5] Both this and P. Oxy. vii. 1007 were classified as Jewish by P. Kahle, *The Cairo Geniza²*, p. 247. I have previously, e.g. in *The Codex*, p. 186 n. 2 and elsewhere regarded the former as Christian, principally because of its format.

blank space, filled in by a second hand in the first of the four instances by κύριος (uncontracted) which also supplied two of the other omissions in the same way. The implication is that the Hebrew Tetragrammaton stood in the exemplar and the first scribe, like the scribe of P. Fouad Inv. 260, either did not know how to write it or was not entrusted with the writing. In the event the second scribe, perhaps not accustomed to writing biblical manuscripts but aware that κύριος was the Greek equivalent of Adonai inserted it here. The text has a number of unique readings which may point to a revision of the LXX.

(2) P. Harris 31 (= H. 148), a small fragment of a papyrus roll with part of Psalm 43, of unknown provenance and assigned to the third or fourth century; θεός was uncontracted. The writing is of the elegant character referred to above.

(3) Stud. Pal. ii. 114 (P. Vindob. G. 35782 = H. 167), two fragments of a parchment roll with part of Psalms 68 and 80 in the version of Symmachus, assigned to the third or fourth century and said to come from the Fayûm or the Heracleopolite. The Tetragrammaton is in the archaic Hebrew characters; the writing is noticeably elegant.

(4) P. Lit. Lond. 211 (= H. 319), a fragment of a parchment roll of Daniel in the version of Theodotion, written in the first half of the fourth century; θεός is uncontracted. This too exemplifies the light and elegant script found in other Jewish texts.

Among texts where the criteria are in conflict and which therefore have a claim to be regarded either as Christian or Jewish the most puzzling is P. Oxy. vii. 1007, part of a leaf of a parchment codex of Genesis dated to the third century. Here the Tetragrammaton appears in the form of a double Yod with a line through it, a form of abbreviation already known from Jewish coins of the second century B.C.; θεός is contracted in the usual way. Thus either we have an instance of a Jewish scribe being influenced by Christian practice or we must assume that a Christian in copying a Jewish manuscript preserved the Hebrew form of the Name, as a few later manuscripts, e.g. the Marchalianus, do. The text, as far as it goes, is that of the LXX. Another text in the same category is P. Oxy. ix. 1166, part of one column of a papyrus roll of Genesis, apparently in the LXX version. κύριος and probably θεός are abbreviated in the usual way; the hand, assigned to the third century is unusually calligraphic, not in what I have called the Jewish style, but a splendid example of Biblical Uncial. It is perhaps more likely to be Christian than Jewish. Other *dubia* are P. Berol. 17213 (= H. 15),[1] part of a papyrus codex of Genesis of the third century in which κύριος is omitted in 19. 19 (though this may be no more than a slip on the part of the scribe),[2] and P. Oxy. x. 1225

---

[1] K. Treu in his article *Christliche Papyri* in *Archiv* 19 (1969), p. 176 classifies this as Christian, but gives no reasons. That ισραηλ and ιερουσαλημ are uncontracted might support but would not prove a Jewish origin.

[2] No *nomina sacra* survive; κύριε (in a secular sense) is omitted at 19.19: see *Archiv* 20 (1970), pp. 46 ff.

(= H. 48), a small fragment of a papyrus roll of Leviticus of the first half of the fourth century, too small for any *nomina sacra* to survive. To this group of papyri may be added the ostracon in Cairo of the late third century (= H. 80) with some verses from Judith.[1]

Treu's list of possible Jewish texts is, naturally enough given his criteria, more extensive than this and includes two which I should place definitely on the Christian side of the line, the Yale Genesis (= H. 12) and the fragment of a second century Psalter in the Bodleian (= H. 151). With the former it is not just the codex form which points to a Christian origin, but the fact that the numeral 318 is written not in words but in symbols, contrary to the usual practice of Graeco-Jewish manuscripts; moreover, in this passage the symbols had for the author of the epistle of Barnabas a mystical significance which the words could not have conveyed and it is reasonable to think that they had the same meaning for the writer of P. Yale I. The second is also a papyrus codex; the editors have restored θεός in an uncontracted form, but given the irregularity of the lines there is no evidence one way or the other.

In addition to the texts of the Old Testament some liturgical papyri of the Roman period have been claimed for Judaism. There can be little doubt of the Jewish origin of the first of them, P. Fouad Inv. 203 (= H. 911), a prayer against evil spirits, written on a roll of papyrus and attributed to the late first or early second century. Both P. Lond. Christ. 5 (= H. 921), a leaf from a liturgical book of the third century, and P. Oxy. xvii. 2068 (= H. 966), some fragments of a papyrus roll of the fourth century, have been thought to be Jewish; but in the latter the contraction of θεός, the eccentric *nomen sacrum* $\overline{\beta c} = \beta \alpha \sigma \iota \lambda \epsilon \acute{\upsilon} s$, and the apparent echoes of Revelation 15: 3 and 1 Timothy 1: 17 in l. 7 render the suggestion doubtful. To these should be added the Vienna text of *The Penitence of Iannes and Iambres*: it was written on the recto of a roll and *nomina sacra* are left uncontracted.[2]

II. *The date of P. Chester Beatty vi (Numbers and Deuteronomy)*

When Kenyon published the fascicle containing the text of P. Chester Beatty vi in 1935, a facsimile of one page having appeared in the General Introduction to the series two years earlier,[3] he had no hesitation in dating the papyrus to the second century and not later than the middle of the century. In this dating he was supported by H. I. Bell, Wilhelm Schubart, and Ulrich Wilcken. A warning note, however, was sounded by A. S. Hunt who, while opining that the hand might be of the second century, remarked that this type of hand

[1] = H. 80.
[2] For this see above p. 63.
[3] E. G. Turner has pointed out that in the companion volume of plates, published in 1958, the reproductions are often reduced in size, whereas that in the General Introduction is actual size.

continued into the third century and that consequently 'late 2nd or early 3rd' would be a cautious date for it. Bell reiterated his support for Kenyon's dating to the mid-second century, with T. C. Skeat's backing, in the introduction to P. Lond. Christ. i and again in his article in the *Harvard Theological Review*. Hunt's comment apart, the dating has not been questioned until quite recently. It is worth observing that neither Kenyon nor any of the scholars he consulted cited a dated text as a parallel to the hand and the only papyrus he adduced in comparison was the London Hyperides. In his copy of the General Introduction (now in the Haverfield Library in the Ashmolean Museum, Oxford) Hunt made a pencilled note to the effect that the hand was 'similar in type to the Oxyrhynchus Genesis (P. Oxy. iv. 656)'. He also underlined in pencil the last six words of Kenyon's statement 'written in a fine hand, of the second century, perhaps of the first half of it'.[1] The Oxyrhynchus Genesis was described by Grenfell and Hunt in their *editio princeps* as being of a 'decidedly early appearance, having in some respects more affinity with types of the second century than of the third', adding that to the latter it should in all probability be assigned. The case for redating this papyrus to the second century was strongly argued by Bell and Skeat in P. Lond. Christ., pp. 6–7.

The general verdict on the date was challenged by E. G. Turner in an article in *Akten XIII. Internat. Papyrologen-kongress*[2] adducing some third-century hands, and subsequently in his *Typology*, pp. 95 and 99. Kenyon (p. ix) well describes the manuscript as 'written in a small, upright hand, square in build (i.e. with height and width of letters about equal), with well-rounded curves and light, flowing strokes'. An important characteristic of the hand (particularly when comparisons are made with hands of the third century) is the way in which the scribe took pains to make all letters, with the inevitable exceptions of ϕ and ψ, of much the same height, even ξ and ρ being usually accommodated within the line and υ being well within it.[3] Only α in one of its two forms is angular; θ and ω are sometimes suspended; υ is made in a single stroke. Ligature and cursive influence are both rare. This rounded Roman hand, while not lending itself to precise definition without a fair number of variations, is familiar enough; it is found both in literary texts and in documents (though the latter will employ more cursive forms than the former) and its origins can be traced in texts of the early second or even the late first century, and it persists into the second half of the third. As seen in P. Chester Beatty vi it is a good, workaday literary hand, if hardly 'a fine example of calligraphy' as Kenyon (p. ix) claimed. The problem is to decide to which stage in the development of the hand this papyrus is to be assigned.

---

[1] Hunt also put a note in his copy of the *Archiv* against Wilcken's article on the Chester Beatty collection (xiii. p. 114), agreeing with Wilcken's comment on the Esther–Daniel–Ezekiel codex that Kenyon's dating was too late. [2] p. 438.
[3] On the principle of bilinearity, i.e. that of working strictly within two notional parallel lines see *GMAW* p. 4 and for a good example from the second century, id. pl. 22.

The origins of the style may be seen in the well-known letter of Gemellus of A.D. 94 (*GLH* 11B), while again among documents early examples of it are *GLH* 13A of A.D. 125, which generally keeps the letters within the line, and Schubart, *Pal.*, Abb. 34, a document of Trajan's reign. On any assessment I should place these documents earlier than P. Chester Beatty vi. Another text, slightly later in date than the Trajanic document, in which some resemblances in letter shapes may be detected is B.G.U. vi. 1210, the Gnomon of the Idios Logos (see above, p. 16), though the writing is less relaxed and the letters are not kept within the line. The development of the style in documents is well illustrated by three Berlin papyri reproduced in U. Wilcken, *Tafeln zur Griechischen Paläographie*; those on pl. XI and XIIa show the mid-second-century form of the hand, that on XIIe that of the early third century; in both the last two the scribe wrote a few lines in a more careful hand before lapsing into his more normal cursive, while another document, reproduced on pl. XIId, of the early third century is written in what is practically a literary hand. Of undated literary texts the Berlin commentary on the Theaetetus (W. Schubart, *Papyri Graecae Berolinenses*, 31), while more regular and freer of cursive influence, has much in common with it.[1] A notable dated example of the style in its later development, if displaying the slight stiffness and formality characteristic of the period, is the Oxyrhynchus fragment of Julius Africanus (*GLH* 27A), written around the middle of the third century.

In his article referred to above E. G. Turner has drawn attention to some third century documents in which he finds parallels to the hand of P. Chester Beatty vi. There are certainly resemblances in some letter shapes both in the edict of A.D. 206 and in the document published by T. C. Skeat and E. P. Wegener in *JEA* 21 (1935); in the former however the hand is less flowing, narrower and more angular, and v and ω are different, while in the latter there is a contrast not found in P. Chester Beatty vi between tall or vertical and other letters; β, it may be noted, is elongated and ϵ straight-backed. These features are still more noticeable in a related text, P.S.I. xiii. 1337 (for the photograph of which I am indebted to Professor Turner); here the rapid, compressed style, particularly noticeable in the ϵ and the μ, contrasts with the flowing, more rounded hand of P. Chester Beatty VI.[2] More to the point is a papyrus to which he has drawn attention in *Typology* (cf. p. 3, with pl. 4b); this document, P. Oxy. xvii. 2105, was dated by Hunt to A.D. 148, but has been convincingly redated on a re-reading of the prefect's name by Dr. John Rea to A.D. 231–6;[3] though letters are

---

[1] The editors of P. Mich. vi observe (p. 86) that the hand of the Theaetetus resembles that of a copy of *Iliad* ii underlying a document of A.D. 215 (P. Mich. vi. 390). This would suggest a date towards the end of the second century for both literary texts.

[2] Turner has subsequently told me (in a letter of 18 July 1977) that he would not wish to press the similarities of this hand too hard and that he regards it as closer to that of P. Chester Beatty i (Gospels and Acts) than to P. Chester Beatty vi.

[3] See P. Oxy. xxxviii. p. xiv.

not kept rigorously within the line and though the ε is either cursive or tall and narrow, the general similarity in style is unmistakeable.

The hand of P. Chester Beatty vi seems to me to belong more naturally to the earlier than to the later stages of the style and if evidence came to light placing it firmly in the second century I should not be surprised; but I know of no dated papyrus that provides a consistently close parallel to this hand and on present evidence a second century date, though possible or even probable, is not necessary and a provisional verdict should be second/third century.

III. *The so-called 'Psalm of the Naassenes' (P. Fayûm 2)*

The only putative manuscript evidence for Gnostic activity in Egypt in the second century (unless the Gospel of Thomas is regarded as Gnostic when P. Oxy. i. 1 might be called in support) is P. Fay. 2 (= H. 1066). This papyrus was found by Grenfell and Hunt at Karanis (Kom Aushîm) in the Fayûm; they described it in their publication as 'a lyric fragment' and dated it to the latter part of the second century.

Shortly after its publication O. Swoboda, acting on a suggestion of W. Crönert, claimed it[1] for a Gnostic Psalm descriptive of Christ's descent into hell, a lost section (in his view) of the Naassene Psalm quoted by Hippolytus (*Ref.* v. 10). By theological scholars this identification has been widely accepted without further examination,[2] but it rests on a very slender foundation.

The hymn or Psalm quoted by Hippolytus is basically pagan and has been superficially Christianized; in its original form (perhaps that of a hymn to Attis) it was assigned by Reitzenstein to the beginning of the second century, though A. D. Nock has suggested that it may be later.[3] There is no overlap and no verbal coincidence between the papyrus and the Psalm; moreover, the latter is not known to be incomplete, and Swoboda's inference from the last verses quoted by Hippolytus—Τὰ κρυπτά τε τῆς ἁγίας ὁδοῦ γνῶσιν καλέσας παραδώσω— that a descent into hell was described in the Psalm is by no means certain. In the text of the papyrus there is no Christian or Jewish reference whatsoever (and it should be noted that θεός is not treated as a *nomen sacrum*) while the final passage preserved in the papyrus does not suit a Christian context. In this (ll. 34 ff.) the hero upbraids an unknown woman who has deceived and apparently ruined him, and for whose sake he is making the descent.[4] Further, as J. Kroll,[5] who regards the proposed identification as impossible, has pointed out, the passage where the hero asks a deity for entry at a closed door is quite inappropriate in a Christian hymn. Swoboda laid considerable stress on the metrical similarity between the two texts; but, as

---

[1] In *Wiener Studien* 27 (1905), pp. 299–301.
[2] Also by H. J. M. Milne in P. Lit. Lond. no. 240 and others, including the present writer in *The Codex*, p. 192.   [3] *Essays on Religion and the Ancient World*, i, p. 201.
[4] See the discussion by D. L. Page in *Greek Literary Papyri* i (London, 1941), n. 94.
[5] In *Gott und Hölle* (Darmstadt, 1963), p. 76 n. 3.

W. Bauer has observed,[1] the anapaestic is the commonest metre of the imperial age, and affords no basis for the identification.

Classical scholars have for the most part ignored the proposed identification[2] and have placed the fragment where it surely belongs, among the not infrequent descriptions in verse or prose in late classical literature of visits to the underworld.[3]

IV. *Christianity and magic in the papyri*

Among the pre-Constantinian papyri those that have a bearing on this subject may be divided into two groups, those that carry a Christian (or in one case possibly Jewish) text and those with merely a Jewish or Christian reference. The former category provides evidence that Christians in Egypt in the third and early fourth centuries were not above using amulets much as their pagan contemporaries did. Among such texts is probably to be classed P. Oxy. xxxiv. 2684 (= H. 558), a piece of papyrus with some verses from Jude, three on the recto and three on the verso, forming a small single folded sheet rather than part of a miniature codex; the verses are not in sequence and are amateurishly written in a semi-cursive hand. The editors assign it to the third/fourth century, but it could well be later. P. Ant. ii. 54 (= H. 347) consists of a piece of papyrus cut to form a rough rectangle, then folded to form a double leaf, and fastened with string; on it was written part of the Lord's Prayer. The editors suggest that it may have been a toy book made for a child, but the hand as well as other considerations point to it being an amulet. The most interesting papyrus in this group is BKT. viii. 17 (= H. 275) of the early third century; a sheet was cut out from a roll carrying a report of legal proceedings of the late second century and on the verso were written in two columns some verses from Job, the text of the second column being unconnected with that of the first. Both passages contain words of power such as ἄγγελοι θανατηφόροι and παντοκράτωρ; as the editor observes, these and not the text itself were what mattered to the owner as the beginning of the second column in the middle of a sentence shows. In fact the text amounts to a magical invocation for healing. The *nomina sacra* for κύριος, ἄνθρωπος, and οὐρανός shows conclusively that it is Christian, not Jewish. In the same category is P. Yale Inv. 989, now convincingly re-edited by R. W. Daniel in *ZPE* 25 (1977), pp. 145 ff., and identified as a protective charm or φυλακτήριον copied from a handbook of magic; it is dated to the third/fourth century A.D. and the κε̄ in l. 5 characterizes it as Christian.

---

[1] In his edition of the Psalm in E. Hennecke–W. Schneemelcher *The New Testament Apocrypha*, Eng. trans. R. McL. Wilson (London, 1965), pp. 807–8. In this discussion there is no mention of P. Fay. 2.

[2] See the references given by R. A. Pack, *The Greek and Latin Literary Texts from Greco-Roman Egypt*[2] (Ann Arbor, 1965) under no. 1923.

[3] See the texts cited by Page, loc. cit.; another description of a descent to the underworld, possibly Orphic in inspiration, is preserved in P. Bon. i. 4 (cf. for the literature R. A. Pack op. cit. under no. 1801.

Just outside our period is the amulet with the text of Psalm 1. 1, published by A. Traversa in *Miscellanea Beltrami* (= H. 84) and erroneously assigned to the second century.

The second group is of little significance for the history of the Church in Egypt. Egyptian magicians drew indiscriminately on a wide variety of cults, and the presence in a magician's book of a Jewish or Christian divine name or expression may mean no more than that the composer of the text was familiar with it; it implies no adherence to the cult on the part of either composer or user. The great Paris magical papyrus (P.G.M. i–iv = H. 1074–5) contains unmistakeable, if misunderstood, Christian allusions as well as Jewish ones, but they are outnumbered by the Greek and Egyptian elements. (P.G.M. iv occasionally treats θεός and κύριος as *nomina sacra* but they are usually left uncontracted as is Ἰησοῦς Χριστός in ll. 3019 ff.).

The Jewish ingredient in ancient magic was of particular importance (cf. A. D. Nock, *Essays on Religion and the Ancient World*, i, pp. 188–9 and 325) and in some magical texts the reference is more likely to be Jewish than Christian. In the case of P. Harris 55 (= H. 1076) the second century date would suggest a Jewish rather than a Christian allusion in the words from Isaiah 60: 1 which are cited in Matthew 5: 34; P. Merton ii. 58, a love charm of the third century with references to Solomon side by side with Cypris and Adonis, and P. Princ. iii. 159 (= H. 968) of the third/fourth century, an amulet for curing fevers in which the κύριοι ἄγγελοι and Σοφία are invoked, may both be placed in the same class. P. Warren 21 (= H. 1081) might be Jewish or Christian.

V. Nomina sacra: *some eccentric forms*

Some unusual forms of *nomina sacra*, including those of particular significance, have been noted above (p. 39); it may be useful to record some others not relevant to the argument of chapter 2 and mostly not recorded in Paap's lists.

In a papyrus codex of the Epistle of Barnabas to be assigned to the third century (P.S.I. vii. 757, re-edited by R. A. Kraft in *Vigiliae Christianae* 21 (1967), pp. 150 ff. = H. 626) θεός and κύριος appear in the form θ· and κ·, with a suprascript line in only one of the three instances while κύριος is twice found unabbreviated. These forms may be, as Paap has suggested (op. cit., p. 125, n. 5) the result of epigraphic influence; he cites one other instance only of this form of abbreviation, $\overline{X}$ for Χριστός in P. Strass. Inv. 254 (= H. 998), a papyrus of the fourth or fifth century. But it is very doubtful if the reading here is correct; in l. 4 the papyrus is broken off immediately after the $\overline{X}$ and, to judge from other lines, there is room for another letter after the break; we should almost certainly read ιυ̅ χ[υ̅]. This is of some consequence since it is occasionally suggested that the critical signs χ and ⳨ (= χρηστόν or χρήσιμον), for which see *GMAW* p. 17, which are found in the margins of some literary papyri may from time to time have stood for χριστός; it has even been suggested (see J. L. Teicher in the *Journal of Jewish Studies* iii (1952), pp. 128 ff.) that the presence of χ in the margin of the Isaiah scroll is proof of the Christian origin of the Dead Sea Scrolls. With the revision of the Strasbourg text no instance can be found in the papyri of the use of the letter χ in a christological sense.

Some unique forms not recorded in Paap's lists are:

$\overline{\pi\tau\varsigma}$ = πατρός in the Chester Beatty Numbers and Deuteronomy

$\overline{\alpha\nu\theta\rho\omega}$ = ἀνθρώπων in PUG 2 (= H. 221), which also offers the usual $\overline{\alpha\nu\omega\nu}$—an indication of the difficulty of trying to trace manuscript affiliations from the forms of *nomina sacra*.

$\overline{\upsilon\iota}$ in P. Baden 4. 57 (= H. 492), a third century manuscript of Romans.

P. Gen. Inv. 253 (= H. 1130) was published by J. Rudhardt in the *Recueil d'études offert à Bernard Gagnebin* (Lausanne, 1975); whether part of a codex or, more probably, an opisthograph roll, it contains apparently parts of more than one theological text and is written in more than one hand and is to be dated in the third century rather than in the second where the editor places it. In ll. 22 and 25 of the recto the editor reads $\overline{\sigma\sigma}$ = σωτῆρος, an abbreviation without parallel and, if correct, the earliest instance of σωτήρ as a *nomen sacrum*. On the basis of the photograph I should read in l. 22 [ι]$\overline{\eta\sigma}$(ου) for the editor's σ(ωτηρο)ς and in l. 25—though with some hesitation—ὑπὸ τοῦ $\overline{\iota\varsigma}$ for ὑπὸ τοῦ σ(ωτῆρο)ς. The whole text needs revision and further study.

INDEX

I. PASSAGES DISCUSSED

II. PALAEOGRAPHICA

III. GENERAL

ADDENDA

1. pp. 59, 61. B. M. Metzger in *The Early Versions of the New Testament* (Oxford, 1977), p. 115 has drawn attention to an Achmimic codex (for which see also P. E. Kahle, op. cit. i, p. 273) to be dated to the fourth/fifth century which contains Matthew, Luke, and John but omits Mark altogether; he also observes that neither in the Life of Shenute nor in that of Pachomius is there any quotation from Mark.

2. pp. 67 ff. For early Coptic manuscripts of the New Testament see now B. M. Metzger, op. cit. pp. 108 ff. To be added to the list given by P. E. Kahle, op. cit. i, pp. 269 ff. are one manuscript of Matthew and another of Acts both in the Sahidic dialect and both in Berlin, and one of John (P. Mich. Inv. 3521) in early Fayumic.

Of non-Biblical Coptic manuscripts I should place Nag Hammadi Codex III (= Codex I in the classification of J. Doresse) in the earliest group, i.e. *c.* 300: see J. M. Robinson, *The Facsimile Edition of the Nag Hammadi Codices* (Cairo, 1972–) and J. Doresse, *Le Livre sacré du Grand Esprit invisible* in *Journal Asiatique* 254 (1966), pp. 317 ff. (with plates).

A select list of early Coptic codices is also given by E. G. Turner, *Typology*, pp. 137 ff.

3. pp. 70–1. If, as seems very probable, Panopolis was the provenance of the Bodmer papyri, it may well have been a centre where pagan, orthodox, and Gnostic cultures all flourished, cf. G. D. Kilpatrick, *The Bodmer and Mississippi Collection of Biblical and Christian Texts* in *Greek, Roman, and Byzantine Studies* 4 (1963), pp. 33 ff. He points out that the Bodmer Library included Greek classical as well as Greek Christian texts, but no Gnostic or other heretical works; he does not refer to the evidence connecting Gnosticism with the area. Cf. also E. G. Turner, *Greek Papyri*, pp. 52–3.

4. p. 76. The exclusive use of the codex form for the Gospels holds only for the canonical gospels; the others are found indifferently in roll or codex.

5. p. 84. To the list of aberrant forms of *nomina sacra* may be added (*a*) ιησους [*sic*] in a parchment roll (l. 101) containing the Greek text of St. Pachomius' letters (see H. Quecke, *Die Briefe Pachoms* (Textus Patristici et Liturgici, fasc. II (Regensburg, 1975)). I should ascribe the manuscript to the later fourth or fifth century. (*b*) In Nag Hammadi Codex III (see above) a line is drawn over ιχθυς on p. 69, l. 15 and also above the letters οσιηλ on p. 62, l. 16; whether this is the name of an angel or there is some confusion with $\overline{ιηλ}$ is uncertain.